What Would Barbra Do?

Emma Brockes

BLACK SWAN

TRANSWORLD PUBLISHERS
61–63 Uxbridge Road, London W5 5SA
A Random House Group Company
www.rbooks.co.uk

WHAT WOULD BARBRA DO?
A BLACK SWAN BOOK: 9780552773188

First published in Great Britain
in 2000 by Bantam Press
a division of Transworld Publishers
Black Swan edition published 2008

Addresses for Random House Group Ltd companies outside the UK
can be found at: www.randomhouse.co.uk
The Random House Group Ltd Reg. No. 954009

The Random House Group Limited supports The Forest Stewardship
Council (FSC), the leading international forest certification organisation.
All our titles that are printed on Greenpeace approved FSC certified paper
carry the FSC logo.
Our paper procurement policy can be found at
www.rbooks.co.uk/environment

Typeset in Minion by
Kestrel Oast Graphic Art Ltd.

Printed in the UK by CPI Cox & Wyman, Reading, RG1 8EX.

2 4 6 8 10 9 7 5 3 1

Mixed Sources

For Adi

CONTENTS

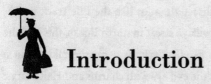

Introduction

What Would Barbra Do?

To give you an idea of the scale of what we are dealing with here, I'd like to begin with an act of superstition. When I was in my teens, I used to babysit for a family who lived across the street from us. The walk from our house to theirs took approximately twenty seconds, during which time it was my mother's habit to stand at the gate and ward off predators with a type of maternal sonar she called 'singing me across the road'. Unlike regular sonar, the sound waves in my mother's version were audible to the human ear and arranged in a pattern that sounded, on a good day and with the wind in the right direction, a lot like the title track to *The Sound of Music*. In our quiet village street in north Bucks, this had the power to disable passers-by as effectively as a missile taking out a warship. Some people see off the evil eye with charms and Hail Marys. My mother did it with show tunes.

The weird thing is, she didn't particularly like *The Sound of Music*. She thought it over-long and sentimental. All things being equal she'd rather have sung something lingering and tragic – 'Ol' Man River', say – or else a breezy number from the 1930s. But she recognized the power of brand awareness and of taking people by surprise and for that she needed a song that everyone, even a mugger, knew hadn't been written with Buckinghamshire in mind.

When I didn't feel like babysitting, I called my friend Deniz to fill in. She lived two streets away and would usually drop in for tea before starting. One summer evening she called around and after we'd chatted in the kitchen for a bit, my mother and I walked her up the path to the gate. We lingered there awhile, as the last of the evening sun backlit the trees and the sound of people playing tennis floated over from the club next door. As Deniz lifted the latch, I said, 'Ma.'

Too late. Too late the realization of what was coming; too late to fall to the ground or ask my mother for a cigarette or think of anything else radical enough to knock her off course.

'The hills are alive . . .'

The last part of the walk was obscured by foliage and always accompanied, through the leaves, by the dying strains of the opening line.* On the doorstep the father of the family would hold eye contact for a second longer than was necessary to acknowledge that yes, beyond the hedge a heart was being blessed with *The Sound of Music*; and no, we weren't going to mention it.

Around that time a 'personal safety adviser' came to the school, to tell us how to repel a potential rapist or mugger. If screaming, biting and kicking failed, we were to do something unexpected, she said, like vomit. This brought the house down, as you can imagine. But looking back I can see that *The Sound of Music* was my mother's gag reflex. If a real mugger had ever materialized, he could probably have done her for excessive use of force.

A decade or so after being sung across the road, I started receiving phone calls from people I hadn't heard from in a while.

'Hi, Emma, it's X.'

* I explain in the penultimate chapter why, due to the unique position *The Sound of Music* occupies in popular culture, this line was an effective deterrent.

'X? Wow. I haven't spoken to you for ages. How are you?'

'Fine. Listen: is it true?'

I was a journalist by then, living in London. I don't know how word got out; through my best friend, I suspect, since one of the callers was her sister-in-law's then partner. It was she who, when I told her I was interviewing Julie Andrews, went quiet for a long time and eventually said, 'But once you've met her, what will you have to look forward to in life?'

Since my babysitting days I had associated *The Sound of Music* with a violent urge to kill someone, but I didn't blame Julie Andrews for this. I had loved her in *Mary Poppins*, so much so that it seemed inconceivable that she might, actually, exist, a real person with contractual obligations to promote the film *The Princess Diaries II*. The people who called me in advance of the interview didn't want anything specific, certainly not autographs. It was more like an act of tenderness towards the memory of themselves as children and a demonstration of the fact that, no matter how old they were, a small part of them would always believe that only Julie Andrews could save them.

'Give Julie our love,' they said, in little voices, and after we'd been introduced in the hotel suite in Park Lane, I did.

'Everyone sends their love,' I said.

'Aaah,' said Julie. 'That's so nice. Tell them I'm *very* grateful.'

From a purely journalistic point of view it is never a good idea to interview someone you have an interest in persuading to like you. This isn't usually a problem; most people above a certain level of prominence are mad as bats. (I recall sitting backstage in a tent in California listening to the soul singer James Brown explain how the American government was trying to eradicate him and, some months later, Jane Fonda describing how the vestibule of her apartment had been designed to look like the female reproductive system.) If Julie Andrews belonged in this category, however, I couldn't see it. What I saw was Poppins, barely – sinisterly, some might say – changed since she leaned out of the window and sang 'A Spoonful of Sugar' to that mechanical robin. Her teeth gleamed. Her eyes sparkled. Her words were like beads of mercury: they didn't run together. When she enunciated 'ex-spouse', in reference to her first husband, it was with a pause in the middle to distinguish the two S sounds.

I had intended to ask lots of searching questions about her allegedly difficult marriage to the director Blake Edwards. But each time I turned down the slip road in that direction, I was flagged down by outriders from my own subconscious screaming, 'What? You're going to insult Julie Andrews? After all these years? *Julie Andrews?* After she reunited the Banks family and defeated the Nazis? Have you *totally* lost your mind?'

And so, I spent most of the forty-minute interview pursuing exclusive angles on just how great she was.

When it was over, Andrews gave me a hug and I returned to the office. I sat down at my desk. I logged on to my computer. Then I cleared my throat and made an announcement. 'I need you all to know that the last person I hugged was Julie Andrews.'

A neighbouring colleague picked up the phone, punched in an internal number and barked, 'Get up here, NOW.'

'Oh my God,' said another.

They rose as one and, without saying another word, formed a small queue beside my desk. I rolled up my sleeves. 'What's this?' said a passer-by on the way to the printer.

'Last person to hug her was Julie Andrews.'

'Fucking hell. Can I join?'

If life was a musical, it is at this point that the room would have transformed into a place of magical possibility: the obituaries desk would have thrown page proofs in the air singing It's So Fab To Be On The Slab! The tea trolley would have sailed in, scattering confectionery, while the subs sang Sport Have Nicked All The Quavers, There Are Only French Fries L-e-e-eft. A chorus of leading left-wing thinkers would have appeared to sing Could This Be The End? (of the Public Sector As We Know It). I dispensed small, heartfelt hugs until we judged the magic Julie dust to have run out. Then we sighed and went back to work.

You can complain about lack of realism and sentimentality; you can complain about bad scripts and shoddy sets. You can love them or hate them, but you can't deny their power. They are there, somewhere, hard-wired to your brain. Isn't it time you asked why?

One final example:

Several years ago I threw a party in my flat in Islington, to which lots of people came. For the first half of the evening we danced and sang to credible chart hits including Public Enemy's 'Rebel Without A Pause' and Destiny's Child's 'Survivor'. A while after midnight, someone sneaked out of the classified part of my music collection the soundtrack to *Fiddler on the Roof*. The effect it had on the party was instantaneous. Suddenly everyone was doing Topol impressions, even the management consultants who had no idea who he was. *Fiddler* was snatched off and replaced with *Cabaret*, which was replaced with the soundtrack to *Mary Poppins*. A discussion kicked off, led by my friend Jim, about what the film actually meant. Jim thought *Mary Poppins* encouraged the view that the only legitimate role for women is a domestic one. I disagreed and argued that *Poppins* was a reminder that feminism begins at home; it's no good Mrs Banks being a suffragette outside the house if she allows her husband to walk all over her at home. My friend Elaine said she thought *Poppins* was an allegory of the crucifixion, knocked back another shot and sank slowly to the floor.

It wasn't until halfway through Jim's exegesis of 'Feed the Birds' (briefly: that it's not a song about pigeons, but about a woman for whom both the state and the community have failed to provide) that I noticed a girlfriend, Alex, eyeing him in a new light across the breakfast bar. Before Jim could finish condemning the anti-vagrancy laws of the 1900s, she had pounced on him, throwing them both backwards into a chair, while over their heads I screamed, 'Brought together by the power of Julie.'

My friend James recently sent me an email (subject line 'I like chess. The game. And cats. The animal') helpfully outlining what he, as a straight man who hates musicals, would like to read in this book: *Starlight Express* as an allegory of the crumbling rail infrastructure of the 1980s; *Rent*, 'despite being dreadful for the non-musical fan', as post-HIV tolerance and sexuality in the 1990s; *Chess* as cold-war politics in the 1970s; *West Side Story* as mass immigration in the American '50s. 'We read about the riots in continental theatres upon the first performance of *The Rite of Spring*, or the strong reaction against Schoenberg's modernism. Were musicals ever taken this seriously, or were they always fluffy fun for tourists, women and gay men?'

Well, I'm all for Schoenberg and his modernism. And I don't intend to shy away from controversy (preview: I never really liked *Grease*). As James suggests, there are good points to be made about how, under cover of lightness, musicals can tackle sacred cows more effectively than other art forms – can be 'fluffy fun' and still merit serious regard. At the same time though, I think something is serious if it is loved, and they are loved, so much so that they can slay imaginary muggers and make people who have only just met fall into each other's arms. I am reminded of the time the great Broadway producer Hal Prince turned to Cameron Mackintosh after seeing *Cats* for the first time and said, 'It's about Queen Victoria, right? It's about Disraeli, right? It's about politics, right?'

'No,' said Mackintosh. 'It's about cats.'

Magic Moments

What Would Barbra Do?

Two summers ago, I flew from London to LA to interview a man called Lemmy. Lemmy, if you are as unfamiliar with him as I was, is the lead singer of Motorhead, a heavy metal band that sold a lot of records in the 1970s, mainly to boys in black T-shirts with the arms cut out of them and girls with Manson Family hairdos. I say heavy metal; for all I know it is thrash metal that Motorhead does, or death metal: in any case it is the sort of metal that sounds like two trains crashing and is guaranteed, as Lemmy puts it, to 'make your lawn die' if it moves in next door to you.

I was not an obvious choice for the job.

We had agreed to meet at the Rainbow Bar and Grill on Sunset Boulevard, where Marilyn Monroe met Joe DiMaggio and which the night before the interview I visualized as a cocktail lounge, with dim lighting and velvet booths and wraith-like serving staff who communicated telepathically to avoid disturbing the *talent*. I wondered what they would make of Lemmy. I had read that he collected Nazi memorabilia and his latest album, *Inferno*, was basically a list of all the people who he thought might want to kill you, among them the devil and unspecified men on horseback. 'No mercy / We bring the sword.'

On a piece of A4 paper I wrote: where is metal music going? How does the new metal compare to the old metal? Is metal misunderstood as an art form?

The next morning I stood in the pearly LA light outside a locked, distressed-looking bar, where the hoarding on the wall advertised a band called Sick Sex, featuring a half-naked woman with the word Slayer written across her torso in black marker pen. 'They're shut?' said Lemmy. 'Oh, fuck.' And taking down two chairs from a table on the terrace, he gave the photographer a hundred-dollar bill and sent him to buy Jack Daniel's and ice and whatever I was drinking – 'Coke.' '*Coke?*' 'Er, vodka and Coke' – from an off-licence round the corner.

I liked Lemmy. He had lived in LA for fourteen years, but still sounded like a comedian on the northern pub circuit. He never had a hangover because he was never entirely sober. 'People don't know how to be outrageous any more,' he growled, pointing to a corner of the terrace where, in days gone by, he recalled couples having sex in full view of the bar. Lemmy looked wistful, then cross. 'If you tried that now the feminist people would go fucking nuts.'

At some point in the interview I let my eyes wander to the outside wall of the bar, where a heavy metal hall of fame had been hung. Lemmy followed my gaze. He asked how many figures on it I could name. Alice Cooper. Steve Tyler. Ozzy Osbourne. I was doing pretty well. 'Who's that?' said Lemmy, pointing to a man with a spray of 1980s hair.

'Don Johnson?'

'For fuck's sake. David Lee Roth.' He looked at me suspiciously. 'What kind of music do you listen to?'

There was a pause. It seemed to go on for some time.

What kind of music do you listen to?

Over the previous fifteen years, there had only been one, brief period when I could have answered this question with anything approaching the truth. That was in early 1996 when I was at university and something called lounge music came briefly back into fashion. It was driven by a kitsch cover band called Mike Flowers Pops and the album *Music to Watch Girls By*, a bunch of easy listening tunes used mainly in jeans ads and promoted as chill-out music for people who would otherwise be listening to skinny white men singing plaintively about their girlfriends. They took up 'lounge' as you might take up something called 'crap' – to show how their patronage could make even the most unpromising material cool.

Lounge music was not very interesting. It was half pastiche, half dim marketing exercise. It threw together mad compilations on the basis that all music made pre-1965 was pretty much the same. But it was the closest the top 40 had come to my record collection in a long time and I could've pulled off fake interest in it without too much effort, just as in 1985 I had been a fake A-Ha fan, in '86 a fake Michael Jackson fan, in '87 a fake Jesus and Mary Chain fan, in '88 a fake INXS fan and even at one stage, in the early '90s, a fake heavy metal fan, buttressing queries about my music taste with the mighty, conversation-stopping word 'Sepultura'. According to *Kerrang!* magazine, Sepultura was 'Brazil's biggest metal band', an impressive fact to wheel out under music taste interrogation, except when you confused 'Sepultura' with 'Scarabeya'. Scarabeya was not Brazil's biggest metal band; it was my friend Sophie's brother Richard's metal band, which played in school halls around the Aylesbury and Stoke Mandeville area.

'What?'

'Scarabeya. The metal band. You know. From Brazil. That sort of thing.'

I pirated every top 40 album that the village library stocked and played them in my sleep. I listened to Radio 1 before school in the morning and taped endless compilations off the chart show on Sunday nights. Some of the music I genuinely liked (not the Jesus and Mary Chain, obviously) and there was an extended period of Stock Aitken and Waterman worship that I thankfully grew out of, otherwise this book would be about Big Fun. And yet, as I laboured over my stereo in flagrant breach of British copyright law – this passed for rebellion in the Home Counties – it was just no good. Nothing took and the voices in my head kept whispering: 'Easy listening is good, easy listening is *goooood*.' Cursing, I dragged myself back to Bing Crosby's 1932 version of 'Buddy Can You Spare A Dime' and the soundtrack to *The Band Wagon*.

When 'lounge music' came back into fashion, therefore, I should have enjoyed a brief period in the sun. At last I knew something that other people wanted to know. I knew the difference between stage and film versions of songs, when they were written and who by. I knew that the 1946 non-musical version of *The King and I* was called *Anna and the King of Siam* and starred Rex Harrison and Irene Dunne, who also played Magnolia in the 1936 version of *Show Boat*. I knew that 'Big Spender' had been a hit for Peggy Lee two years before Shirley Bassey got hold of it and that it had come from the 1966 stage musical *Sweet Charity*. I knew which songs

Frank Sinatra shouldn't have recorded. But as it turned out, none of this mattered.

It was a bit like when flares came back in the late 1990s; if you tried to wear your parents' originals from the '70s they looked more tragically out of kilter with the times than the skinniest drainpipes. Where there was at least some logic to the way fashion grew up out of itself, however, there was no logic to the new lounge music. I found myself getting uptight about authenticity. What, I asked, picking up an album from a modish friend's CD rack, was Petula Clark doing on the same album as Vic Damone? What had Don McLean to do with Dusty Springfield? And why was '60s Britpop being shoved in alongside '40s big band? For God's sake, what was Andrew Lloyd Webber doing there? She looked at me as if ectoplasm had started dribbling out of the side of my mouth, but it was no good. Trying to go along with this stuff was harder than pretending to like the Shamen in '91. I had some pride. I was not a fake lounge fan.

Lemmy kept steady eye contact from beneath the rim of his cowboy hat. The moles on his face were the size of toadstools and his skin was very pale. Oh well, I thought. What the hell.

'Mostly show tunes,' I said.

Behind me, the photographer gasped. ('Rap music,' he lied, the little creep, when the question came his way. Well, I've seen the CDs in his car and have two words for him: soft soul.)

'Beg your pardon?' said Lemmy.

'Mostly show tunes,' I said.

'What,' he said, 'Andrew Lloyd Webber?' I made a face. 'Oh, she turns up her nose at Andrew Lloyd Webber.' He sipped his bourbon. '*Oklahoma!*?'

'Yes.'

'*South Pacific*?'

'Yes.'

'*The Sound of Music*?'

'Sort of.'

Lemmy looked at me, a long, hard look. 'You deserve to be nailed to the fucking cross.'

It might be useful at this stage to clarify what I mean by musicals. By musicals, I don't mean *Riverdance*. I don't mean *The Waltons* or *The Bridges of Madison County*. I don't mean Alma Cogan, Cliff Richard, Perry Como, Val Doonican, Daniel O'Donnell's 'Irish Christmas', Stevie Wonder's easy listening version of 'Blowin' in the Wind', Werther's Originals or *Songs of Praise*. I don't mean any of the Ovaltiney horrors which, when I worked in my teens on hospital radio, poured in as requests from the geriatric wards and we called Music to Die To, along with Jim Reeves's 'The Old Rugged Cross' and anything by Pat Boone. (I realize that I am doing to fans of Pat Boone here what Lemmy did to me; but you have to draw the line somewhere.)

I don't even mean films or stage productions in which the characters sing at each other instead of speaking. *Gone With the Wind* is truer to the spirit of what I mean than *The Phantom of the Opera*. A friend of mine – in fact, the only friend of mine who shares my taste to the same degree – has learned over the years to summarize her position in the chat-up line, 'Do you like the 1940s?' (As a result she has kissed a lot of odd-looking men who know who Carol Channing is.) I know what she means; it's a certain sharpness of style, a perfectly balanced combination of cynicism and romance that covers all eventualities. But it's more than that, too. When I was a child it had to do with the magic of a world so far removed from my own that it shimmered in my mind like a mirage. When I was an adolescent it had to do with ambition, the link established in all those backstage musicals between hard work and reward. While pop music in the early '90s glamorized ugly blokes from Manchester pissing their talent up the wall, musicals glamorized nerdiness – it probably doesn't need to be pointed out at this stage that I was quite nerdy. It had to do with perversity, too. I have no doubt that, had I actually been growing up in the 1930s or '40s, I would have been grooving to turn of the century beats.

Whatever their individual faults or merits, the important thing is that you always come away from a true musical with the unshakeable feeling that it is *on your side*. I can't quite put my finger on it, but it is related in some mysterious way to Shirley Bassey standing alone on stage dressed head to toe in mink singing 'I Who Have Nothing'. You know?

A musical rises or falls on its ability to find that magic moment – snap! – when the hairs on your neck stand up like iron filings and all the dreary elements of your life are either banished or transformed into material for an epic, noble suffering. This isn't brought about by noisiness – despite all the hollering, there are no magic moments in *Chicago*, except maybe the bit when Catherine Zeta Jones looks at the camera and spits that she's no one's wife but still loves her life with such aggression Michael Douglas should worry. The magic moment isn't necessarily the same as the musical's most famous scene, either. In *Fame*, it's not the dancing in the street that gives you chills so much as the opening sequence, when poor Doris Finsecker recites the lyrics to 'The Way We Were' while her brother accompanies her on the piano and tears pour down her strange mother's cheeks.

In *The Sound of Music*, the magic moment isn't the opening scene when Julie Andrews glides across the Alps, arms outstretched and with a look on her face that is only fully explained when you know she was being filmed at close range from a helicopter. *The Sound of Music*'s real killer moment creeps quietly up two-thirds in, when, having fired Maria for recycling his curtains and falling in the lake, Captain von Trapp hears singing in the house and storms off to investigate. (She looks at his retreating back the way Jesus did on the market place.) Marching into the house, he finds his children in the parlour, singing the title song to the baroness. 'The hills are alive . . .'

As he listens in the doorway, something begins to dawn on him. Yes, he thinks, I remember this, the tender feelings provoked by a seven-part harmony. An expression breaks across the captain's face and as the ice round his heart melts tears spring to his eyes and he walks into the room crooning that he, the captain, also goes to the hills when his heart is lonely. The children stare at him as if a small mammal has just appeared through the curtain of his fringe, but, recovering themselves, come in with backing vocals to accompany their father in the first von Trapp family singalong since the death of the mother and at *that* moment, brrr, click, the baroness is defeated, a chill goes through the audience, Maria has brought music back into the house! And that, my friends, is the magic of the musical.

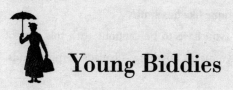 **Young Biddies**

What Would Barbra Do?

In 1994, I went to university. *Evita* hadn't come out yet, so the last memory anyone had of a film musical was the 1980 Olivia Newton John/Gene Kelly disaster, *Xanadu*. Judging musicals on the basis of *Xanadu* is a bit like judging rock music on the basis of Slade's 1985 *The Slade Christmas Party Album*, so there was still some need for discretion. One evening, I was in the pub with a group of friends when the Carpenters came on the jukebox. Everyone mocked their morbid crooning; everyone except one girl.

'Actually,' she said, 'I quite like this stuff.'

'What stuff?' I said (you have to be cautious with this sort of statement; she could have meant anything – ballads, family bands, carpentry).

'Old stuff.'

'Yeah? Like what?'

'Frank Sinatra.'

'Yeah?'

'Musicals.'

'Yeah?'

'Yeah. But nothing post '71. It all went wrong after *Fiddler on the Roof*.'

The Young Biddy movement, as Adi and I came to call ourselves, was a movement of two. We were by necessity underground, listening in company to St Germain and the Chemical Brothers, circulating, in secret, bootleg copies of *My Fair Lady* (the pre-dubbed Audrey Hepburn mix) and French language versions of 'Where Have All the

Flowers Gone?' ('Qui Peut Dire Où Vont Les Fleurs?'). Our manifesto recognized that:

- the contribution made by Angela Lansbury to Broadway and film musicals, 1946–71, was in many ways superior to her work as Jessica Fletcher on *Murder, She Wrote*.

- the deletion of key scenes from *The Way We Were* irrevocably damaged the film.

- Audrey Hepburn's cockney accent in *My Fair Lady* was every bit as bad as Dick Van Dyke's in *Mary Poppins*.

- 'White Christmas' was not written by Isaiah Berlin.

- With the size of his over-bite, Howard Keel was lucky to have hit the big time.

- Bing Crosby was like the easy listening version of Chucky, stalking our nightmares with his pipe and his fawn cardigan.

- The first ten minutes of *The Sound of Music* are equal to any artistry since Plato's *Republic* but still

make you want to hide your face, like seeing the
hand of God.

– *Mary Poppins* is by and large the better film.

– The choice of Betty Hutton to replace Judy Garland in
the 1950 film version of *Annie Get Your Gun* was
misguided to the point of criminal insanity.

– No matter how dire the situation, it is never beyond
the redemptive reach of a Rodgers and Hammerstein
show tune.

Young Biddyism involved knowing things that no under-25 at
the time should have known. We could list Frank Sinatra's wives,
like Henry VIII's, in chronological order and with the fate that
befell each of them. We argued late into the night over whether
the video for Michael Jackson's 'Thriller' was inspired by the
graveyard dream sequence in *Fiddler on the Roof* and whether it
was true that when Gene Kelly invited people to his house in Malibu,
he forced them to play beach volleyball. We'd *start* watching *Gone
With the Wind* after midnight. Once, Adi bought *Hits from the Blitz:
The Best of Vera Lynn* from a mainstream record store in broad
daylight.

There was room within the movement for differences. Adi was
committed to the Ginger Rogers 'it takes a lot of brains to be this

dumb' send-up of the Hollywood heroine, which she felt rescued the genre from sickliness. In principle I agreed with her. But I'd had the misfortune to catch Rogers on *Wogan* in the mid-1980s and couldn't shake the memory of her bloated face and those startled, kewpie-doll eyes, which beneath the polite banter seemed to be screaming, 'Help! Get me out! I'm trapped in the body of a hideous old woman and I can't find the exit!'

My preference was for the 1950s and those thunderous, three-hour extravaganzas which tortured our Sunday afternoons as kids. I liked the colour and the high drama and the sense that there was more going on in them than at first appeared – the twitch of an eyebrow during a sappy song or the suggestion, in the rouge on the leading man's cheeks, that his interests lay wide of the heroine's eyes. Above all else, I was a tragedy fan. If a woman wasn't standing alone at the end of the film, lit by a spotlight and bench-pressing twice her own body-weight in grief, I could take it or leave it. Yeah, I thought, walking through Oxford with the pained expression of the misunderstood visionary; that's how it is; we all die alone in the end.

After university I moved to London. For three years I shared a flat with a male friend, first above a busy junction in Camden and then opposite a park in Islington. We bought a PlayStation, an electric piano, an electric guitar, an amp, speakers and a thing for destoning olives. We propped a life-sized cardboard cut-out of the Spice Girls that we'd found in the street against the kitchen wall. We stayed up till 3 a.m.

watching horror films on Channel 5 and got spots and mild salt poisoning from all the ready meals we ate. Neither of us could cook so, when we weren't caning the microwave, we went out for dinner and let the kitchen turn into an open landfill. For weeks not so much as a sweet wrapper was thrown away. Eventually, while scavenging for snacks one day, my flatmate dipped his hand into a bag of potatoes that had been sitting by the door for the best part of a year. I heard the scream from downstairs.

'What?' I tore into the kitchen.

'Maggots!' he cried. He stood nursing his hand to his chest. 'In the potatoes.' He gave me a reproachful look.

'You say that as if it's my fault,' I said.

'It's *both* our faults,' he said.

We cleaned up our act.

There were strict rules regarding the emission of pre-1960s music in the flat. My flatmate's music taste had gone down a fairly traditional route of Pink Floyd to Kiss and Aerosmith, to a revival of electronica, finally settling down, in his early twenties, to a stable diet of indie rock. He flinched when I used his £3,000 stereo, bought in the Gray's Inn Road after months of deliberating over speaker quality and something called aluminium cone diaphragms, to play music with titles such as 'June is bustin' out all over' and 'When I marry Mr Snow'.

'See?' I said.

'What?' he said.

We held periodical education sessions, to try better to understand each other's taste.

'Judi Dench can't really sing but it doesn't matter because Sondheim wrote the song for a non-singer.'

The natural response to this would be: my God! Sondheim wrote 'Send in the Clowns' for a non-singer? What was he, *insane*? That's outrageous! Who the hell was it? (Glynis Johns. 'Send in the Clowns' has no sustained notes at the end of each phrase.)

'But it's shite,' said Jat and put on *Still Got the Blues* by horrible old rocker Gary Moore. I tried to convince him that musicals were getting more credible by the day and that the Buzzcocks' '77 hit 'Ever Fallen in Love' was inspired by a line from *Guys and Dolls*. But he wasn't having it. Eventually we agreed to a time-share arrangement with the caveat that, since it was his stereo, I would promise never to play anything by Barbra Streisand while he was in the flat.

There are occasional advantages to having bad taste. (I use 'bad' here in the same way Margaret Thatcher used 'terrorists' to describe the ANC.) I was walking down Upper Street in north London one day when one of those out of work actors hired by charities to charm your credit card details from you threw himself in my path. 'Hey you.' He pointed to my headphones. 'Whatchyou listening to?'

He had that look they all have, that come on baby, you know you can't resist me look that makes me want to push them into traffic. He waggled his clipboard.

'Whatchyou listening to?'

'Vera Lynn,' I said. '"The Anniversary Waltz", and like the precious few seconds bought by the heroine of a horror movie after throwing hot water in her assailant's eyes, his momentary confusion allowed me to body-swerve the clipboard and continue on my way.

'The Anniversary Waltz' was on a CD originally given to me as a joke, but which turned out to be quite good. It was followed, on random play, by Vince Hill's terrible version of 'Edelweiss'. Hill was a stowaway who got onto my system via a compilation I bought for the song 'True Love', the Bing Crosby/Grace Kelly duet from *High Society*, and which I thoughtlessly uploaded in its entirety so that now not only Hill but Alma Cogan, Bobby Darin, Matt Monro and Helen Reddy doing 'I Don't Know How To Love Him' from *Jesus Christ Superstar* come around with depressing regularity. Like a lot of bad theatrical singers, Hill confuses slurring with pathos. I could have taken him off my playlist, but if you actually liked every song you had on iTunes, it would take all the suspense out of random play.

When you have a music collection like mine on your iPod, you have to keep a steady finger on the volume control when you're out in public. I recall a sticky moment when the engines of the train died suddenly just as Ethel Merman was reaching her climax in 'Rose's Turn'; she sings so loudly and with such wayward vibrato that you worry she's going to derail from the tune entirely and turn into a police siren. I have stood next to middle-aged men with soft rock bleating from their headphones and this sucky look on their faces that you know, you just *know* means they're pretending that their journey to work is going out live on E4.

Young Biddies

It's amazing how unprotective people are of vulnerabilities like this. If your idealized version of life has a Dido soundtrack, do you really want everyone on the Central Line at rush hour to know about it?

'Fagin was a kiddy fiddler,' I said to Adi one day.

She was idling on the sofa in a patch of late afternoon sunlight. The floor was strewn with newspapers and the debris from lunch.

'No he wasn't,' she said. 'He was a kindly old gentleman.'

'Yeah, right,' I said. 'He called the boys "my dears". He was a creep.'

'You're wrong. He was a rogue, but he wasn't a paedo. "No violence, Bill, no violence."'

'Man. You need to review the situation.'

'You're just fucking wrong.'

She was about to head off for a three-month backpacking tour of China and had come to my flat for the send-off. Over the years our choice of material for these send-offs would refine until we had worked out a watertight programme that could be drawn on in the case of abduction, hospitalization or imprisonment, to get one through the ordeal. Any musical made post-1971 was automatically thrown out as unworthy and that included Lloyd Webber, the '70s rock musicals and, yes, *Fame*. It was our feeling that, while individual songs in these productions were often brilliant, taken as a whole the shows were uptight and humourless, paving the way for the sort of Pop Idol rictus that mistook vocal perfection for genuine feeling, a kind of stage-school singing prefigured by Sarah Brightman in her performance in *The Phantom of the Opera*. Sarah Brightman sent shivers down one's spine, but of the wrong kind.

That first time, for pure, undiluted joy, we played the 'Who Will Buy' number from the DVD of *Oliver!*.

'Is that Barry Gibb?' I said. (If you look carefully during the milkmaids/flower-sellers/window-cleaners' chorus, there is a fleeting shot of a bearded man playing a woodwind instrument up a tree. We rewound and freeze-framed.)

'No. Nancy isn't actually dead at the end,' said Adi.

'Are you insane? Of course she's dead. She's just been clubbed over the head with an iron bar.'

'Her legs are still twitching.'

'You are so unbelievably wrong I can't understand how we've been friends all these years.'

(On further investigation: there is actually a death twitch – her legs spasm once – but the reaction of the bystanders suggests all hope is lost. No one runs for an ambulance.)

We played the standoff in *Whatever Happened to Baby Jane?* ('but you are in that wheelchair, Blanche') and Melanie's deathbed exit from *Gone With the Wind*. From *The King and I* we played the key change in Yul Brynner and Deborah Kerr's performance of 'Shall We Dance' and did karaoke to his death scene.

'Mrs Anna,' I said. 'You do not understand. He is dying.'

'Dying?' Adi replied. 'The King? Oh, no, Lady Thiang, what happened?'

I sighed. 'Who can say what it is that makes a man die?'

Enemies of the genre will call this poor realism, since the King was right as rain and hopping about not five minutes before. Fans of the genre will call it symbolic compression – great truths can sometimes only be conveyed at epigrammatic level. One understands this as one understands a muscle memory, a recognition that this is how it was and had always been.

On screen, Deborah Kerr's English reserve briefly gave way to racking sobs. 'Was he as good a king as he could've been?' Adi asked.

'I don't think any man is as good a king as he could've been,' I replied sadly, through a mouthful of chocolate mousse.

We played the video of *Streisand, Live at the MGM Grand, 1993*, which was like a multi-vitamin supplement, an all-round boost to the immunity. I can't remember who said it first, but I do remember what provoked it. It was that bit in the concert when Streisand duets with a play-back of herself singing 'Piece of Sky' from *Yentl*. Even without the help of half a pint of vodka it is a striking performance, a sort of event horizon of the ego, which, of everything we'd seen that night, we felt sure was the one to get Adi across China. At low points she was to think of this moment and ask herself, 'what would Barbra do?' If the memory of Babs serenading a cinema-sized projection of her own face at ear-bleeding volume didn't lift her spirits, nothing would.

These were the last days of subterfuge. Thanks to Madonna's agreeing to appear in it, the film version of *Evita* made musicals slightly more credible, and then, in 2001, Baz Luhrmann made *Moulin Rouge!*. It featured modern pop songs and modern stars and a modern approach, which is to say a post-modern one. Ewan McGregor and Nicole Kidman performed songs by Elton John, David Bowie and Sting and it didn't really matter that they couldn't sing because it was all so loud and bright and fun. *Moulin Rouge!* was a big hit and made musicals suddenly cool again.

I hated it.

But it did mean that the days of creeping about in the shadows were over. As Gloria Estefan once put it, we were coming out of the dark. Hard on the heels of *Moulin Rouge!* came *Chicago*, then *De-Lovely*, then a new film version of *Rent* and a remake of *The Producers*, then *Wicked*. Bits of modern music started to make their way into my collection, too. Just before he became super-famous I went to Manchester to interview Eminem and to my surprise found that I liked some of his stuff. Each song told a story and although his tone was mocking, he mocked himself and the expectations people had of him and of rap music generally. In a way, it seemed to me, his music was in the best tradition of the musical: that is, a narrative art in which the singer is sincere but at the same time at a slight angle to what he's singing about. When Eminem's film *8 Mile* came out in 2002 it was a more conventional movie musical than had been made for a long time, about a poor boy who dreams of getting into show business and hitting the big time. It even contained the line 'Are you asking me out on a date, Jimmy Smith Jnr?' which sounded like something from *It's A Wonderful Life*.

None of this was ever going to make listening to most of the music

I listened to acceptable. The deep-seam, pre-1940s stuff wouldn't see a revival this side of doomsday. But it did make the concept of musicals seem slightly less freakish and archaic. Oh, and something else that probably helped: I got older.

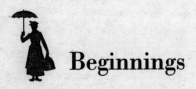

Beginnings

Beginnings

The reason I love musicals is that my mother loved musicals, which is also the reason why, for many years, I couldn't stand them. If the period during which I couldn't stand them had coincided with my adolescence it would have saved me a lot of grief; but the best I could do at that stage was to hate loving them and hope the phase would pass. (The period during which I straightforwardly hated them was between the ages of five and nine, when, uselessly, nobody cares what you love or hate.)

My mother didn't approve of sticking plasters. 'Let the air in,' she said, when I cut my finger as a child, and taught me that children who wore plasters compromised their natural immunity with potentially fatal consequences later in life. She thought that people who ran at the sight of a wasp were not only cowardly, but counter-productive. 'What a performance,' she would say, as they tore off down the garden. It was her contention that only people who made a fuss got stung.

'What a performance.' I didn't know it then, but there was a whole industry committed to promoting this outlook as the only workable way to get through life. My mother came of age when musicals were still mainstream popular culture; it just so happened that they suited her temperament exactly. In glorious Technicolor there was Deborah Kerr in *The King and I*, getting shirty in the face of ineptitude; there was Shirley Jones, carrying herself uncomplainingly through *Carousel*; there was an endless parade of tap-dancing women who could out-dance the tap-dancing men. My mother loved the all or nothing aspect of them, the sheer size of their ambition, the fact that even the silliness – especially the silliness – invited ridicule just to defy it. They willed you with every fibre to believe in them as much as they believed in themselves. This, she thought, was how it should be.

I can't remember the first musical I saw. All I know is that I was still young and pliable enough not to find it strange that the people in it were singing to each other instead of speaking. I was used to this, what with my mother perennially wafting about the house singing 'Sweet Mystery of Life At Last I've Found Thee' and 'I'm Just A Girl Who Can't Say No'. She had no memory for lyrics and only the slightest attachment to the tune. When my mother sang a song, stray bits of other songs would make spontaneous guest appearances in it, especially for some reason the phrase 'holy cow', which had worked its way loose from the chorus of 'If My Friends Could See Me Now' (*Sweet Charity*, 1966) and would turn up all over the place, usually in the title song from *Cabaret*.

'You've got it totally wrong,' I would say.

'Oh, shut up.'

She sang 'No No Nanette' and 'A Funny Thing Happened to Mabel'. She sang rough versions of Sophie Tucker's 'My Yiddishe Momme' and 'I Dream of Jeannie With the Light Brown Hair', which I have just looked up on Wikipedia to find was written by a guy called Stephen Foster in 1854 – it was so much worse than I thought. It was years before I realized just how many of the sayings she used – 'by George, she's got it!', 'doing what comes naturally', 'ah yes, I remember it well' – were not her own, but Alan Jay Lerner's or Irving Berlin's. One came to light just the other day, 'good riddance to bad rubbish', which she would say after a fight with our neighbour about overhanging foliage. It popped up when I was watching the film version of *Sweet Charity*, along with a vision of two women squaring up to each other with secateurs and gardening gloves.

To my mother, musicals were old friends who could always be relied upon to say the right things. They cheered you up when you were down and egged you on when you were miserable and made you feel lighter than air at all stages in between. They were a rare, permissible extravagance: of dress, of movement, of talent, of emotion. Extravagant suffering and extravagant forbearance. What is sadder than a sad song, or happier than dancing? It made no difference if they were light opera or melodrama, from the '30s the '40s, the '50s or the 1960s. It didn't matter how long they were or how ludicrous. I learned to look out for anything with an exclamation mark at the end of it – *Oliver!*, *Oklahoma!*, *Hello, Dolly!* – you could count on losing at least two and a half hours of your afternoon to these babies. It was lost on me how something as compressed as Rossano Brazzi's courtship of Mitzi Gaynor in *South Pacific* ('I am older than you. If we have children and I die, you could afford to take them back to America if you like' – this a few days after meeting her) could at the same time seem so achingly drawn out.

'The most spectacular story ever told, starring Howard Keel as the loving, singing, shooting Frank Butler!' So ran the title in the opening sequence of *Annie Get Your Gun*. Since when is loving, singing and shooting a desirable triptych?

'It's a classic,' my mother said, and dismally I submitted.

What Would Barbra Do?

*

It was my mother who told me about Betty Hutton's last-minute replacement of Judy Garland in *Annie Get Your Gun*. She said Garland was unreliable because people had been unkind to her as a child and made her strap down her boobs and take drugs. 'Never take drugs.' She thought Omar Sharif was sexy. She thought Howard Keel was sexless. She had a beef with Audrey Hepburn for taking Julie Andrews's role of Eliza Doolittle when the stage production of *My Fair Lady* transferred to the screen. Gloria Grahame, she said, was the true star of *Oklahoma!*. Celeste Holm, she said, was the true star of *High Society*. She said that *South Pacific*, despite paying lip service to the idea of racial equality, did wrong by the actress playing Bloody Mary, who unlike her white co-stars died in relative poverty.

My mother said that Lee Marvin had the right idea in *Paint Your Wagon* when he said you had a choice in life, to be a somebody or a nobody. In musicals, nobodies blamed other people for their faults and were punished by drowning or falling to their deaths from the tops of haystacks (if my mother had been a scriptwriter she'd have had them killed fleeing a swarm of wasps). Somebodies were forever finding things to overcome and overcoming them. When I didn't want to go to Brownies, my mother cited the example of Jeanette MacDonald, who, when faced with the unpleasant task of singing opposite Nelson Eddy, didn't make a fuss but gritted her teeth and sang on. Despite a successful partnership spanning almost a decade, MacDonald couldn't stand the sight of Eddy – couldn't stand him! my mother said – but like a trouper ploughed on through storylines contrived to show off her indomitable American spirit. The only thing I remember seeing her in was the film *New Moon* – 'Charles, Charles! You must come back! You must come back to me!' – and that film about the San Francisco earthquake, in which she stands in the ruins of the city with a look of both sorrow and determination on her face and rallies the survivors with her glass-shattering soprano. Judy Garland parodied it in her 1962 stage show, *Live at Carnegie Hall*, singing deliberately off-key and trilling sarcastically, which was to some extent a parody of herself as a graduate of similarly daft musical numbers and may, or may not, have hinted at the despair and self-loathing that would ultimately destroy her.

Brigadoon, my mother told me, had stolen half the budget off *Seven Brides for Seven Brothers* and then put it to thoroughly frivolous use. 'One day,' she said darkly, 'you will see *Brigadoon*, and then you can make up your own mind.'

Most of my friends who like musicals were indoctrinated by their mothers in this way and most of them held out against it, too, until somewhere along the line they saw a film that overcame their resistance. My friend Deniz, who has never entirely recovered from being sung across the road that time, spent the early part of her childhood in Turkey, where her English mother played lots of musicals to her, as a way of reinforcing her English. They were pretty much the only English-language culture she was exposed to and she assumed they were contemporary. It came as a shock, years later, to discover that they were made two decades before she was born and that people in the English-speaking world didn't really flounce about in costumes the size of tents and the colour of traffic lights.

For Deniz, it was *Seven Brides for Seven Brothers*. For me, it was the vision of a woman in a gold-sequined wetsuit and a spray-painted crown. She stood on a trapeze and dived through plumes of red and gold smoke into a tank in which other women floated face down with one leg in the air, like capsized flamingos. Had there ever, in the whole history of the world, been anyone as marvellous as Esther Williams? I saw *Million Dollar Mermaid* when I was nine years old and concluded that the only possible future for me was as one of Billy Rose's aquabelles.

Williams took where the others failed because the world she inhabited was one that to a very small extent I was familiar with. The reality of competitive swimming was a municipal pool where the fumes were like mustard gas and the water like ice; where for an hour before school or after you ploughed up and down trying to keep from getting a mouthful of verruca sock and chipped teeth from the girl swimming in front of you. It was inter-school swimming galas in which the swimmer in the next lane was that beefcake from the convent you always came up against, the one with the black cross printed on her swimming cap, which out of the corner of one eye, as you stood on the starting blocks, looked like a swastika. It was the feeling of terror as you waited for the whistle; the eerie calm of the water; the desire to come first and also not to come first, since coming first meant you would be pressured to sign up for weight training and 'commit' more fully to the team.

Beginnings

It wasn't like that in *Million Dollar Mermaid*. The swimmers in the film had little silk butterflies sewn into their swimming caps. The swimming costumes were gold and rather than racing in straight lines across the pool they used 'all the space available' to them, as my drama teacher would have put it, and flew through the air. Unlike the heroines of other musicals I'd seen, Esther Williams didn't sit around and mope, waiting to get married; she cleaved forcefully through the English Channel in a bathing suit that looked like an iron lung; she dived from amazing heights into tiny tanks; she joined the Navy. In one memorable scene from the film *Easy to Love*, she waterskied across a lake while a helicopter flew overhead, dangling a trapeze, which she grabbed hold of to be hoisted eighty feet in the air and dived off into the middle of a V-formation made up of sixty-eight of the world's greatest waterskiers.

It was of this I was thinking when I climbed the ladder to the top of the diving board at the pool one Saturday. I felt the wind whistling round my ears and the concrete cold beneath my feet. After hesitating for a second, I dived head first in what I hoped looked like a beautiful, gravity-defying swan dive. I hit the water with such a thud that I felt a ripple move up my spine.

'My God,' said my swimming coach when my mother told her what I had done. 'She could have broken her neck.'

Broadway Baby

I was born in London but we moved out when I was two and since my mother had never quite reconciled herself to leaving, we went back up to town a lot, mainly to the theatre.

The best thing about going to the theatre was putting on a black dress and driving up the M4. ('You dress her in black?' said a friend of my mother's, eyeing me with disapproval. My mother smiled back at her, pityingly. She regarded dressing her child in black as just one of the many, small distinctions between herself and other home counties mothers who lacked, as she put it, 'perspective'.) We came in past Northolt Aerodrome, where the street lamps were half height, down Western Avenue and then round the North Circular into town. 'People live here?' I asked. London seemed very big and dark and when we walked from the car to the theatre I held on to my mother's hand. As you approached it from the side street, the theatre sizzled in light.

I recall that *Starlight Express* was very loud. And dark. And that for no good reason the people in it pretended to be trains and flew around a track that wove in and out of the audience while children screamed and – it must have been around the time of the early *Star Wars* films – waved light sabres. In *Oliver!*, the stage was so far away it was like watching a flea circus. A child got into a coffin and couldn't get out again. I wondered how they got the boat to move across the set in *The Phantom of the Opera*. What did he look like under his mask? Was it a birthmark? Or more like the puckered skin interspersed with hard, smooth patches which covered the stomach and legs of my friend Amanda from when she pulled a boiling kettle over herself, the scarring from which was caused not so much by the hot water as by the failure of the supervising adult to remove her clothes instantly, resulting in the adhesion of her dress to her skin and subsequent scene at the hospital in which, according to various reports collated by my mother and passed on to me in thrilling detail, the dress was removed and *the skin came with it*, while Amanda screamed in agony.

In *Wonderful Town* the American accents were off and the leading lady underwent a reversal in her position on romance to the effect 'it's all cobblers, oh hang on, no it isn't, I'm in love'. Even at the age of eight, I thought this sucked.

The most interesting thing about *Joseph and the Amazing Technicolor Dreamcoat* was the discussion we had before going. 'It doesn't sound like our sort of thing,' said my mother, not words she had ever been known to utter about a musical before, but she regarded *Joseph*'s biblical theme as a blasphemy against musical theatre. Still, she agreed to see *Joseph* where *Jesus Christ Superstar* never got off the drawing board. 'Oh no,' she said, 'absolutely not,' as if my dad's offer to get tickets had been code for let's tie our only daughter in a sack and throw her in the canal.

I quite liked *Joseph*. I liked the bit where Benjamin got called a 'nasty youth' and for a while afterwards 'nasty youth' replaced 'elongated monkey' as the funniest word combination in the English language. ('The boy leaped from the train like an elongated monkey' had come up in a book at school and its spin-off insult – 'you're an elongated monkey' – had us rolling in the aisles for weeks.)

We went to a production of *Carmen* at Earls Court that Princess

Anne was at and I spent the whole time looking through opera glasses at a yellow dot in the royal box. A few days afterwards, the toreador song came on the radio during the school run.

'Peanut butter song!' sang my friend Jill.

'Actually,' I squeaked, 'it's from *Carmen*.'

Her mother looked at me in the rearview mirror but said nothing.

When I was about ten, we went to see *42nd Street*. It was a revival of the 1980 stage show which was itself based on the 1933 film, starring Ruby Keeler as the chorus girl who gets a shot at the big time when the star goes over on her ankle ('Oh! My ankle! My ankle!'). The score was by Harry Warren and the dance sequences in the film by Busby Berkeley.

42nd Street is competitive in the way only children, really, understand; pure, undiluted, life or death. The stage show has a *physical* effect on the audience, as fifty tap shoes all dance the same steps and the reverberations kick in at rib-level. There was Peggy Sawyer, having to learn the entire part in one afternoon; there was the old star passing on the baton and telling her to be so swell she'd hate her; saying, in a fit of bravado, how she was glad she broke her damn ankle if it meant she could get out of the big time and find herself a husband and, if she was lucky, a future in vaudeville. There was the director telling Peggy that she had to give and give and go-out-there-a-nobody-but-come-back-a-star. I applied this to every errand I ran from that day forth, which turned buying penny sweets into a performance for the benefit of the talent scout lurking behind the card rack in Bunces.

When you return to *42nd Street* as an adult you notice, with some surprise, that it is very much a film of the Depression; the performers almost kill themselves to keep afloat. Film theorists have read Busby Berkeley's kaleidoscope of girls as the visual representation of how capitalism works, interchangeable units fluctuating on a production line while the individual up front gets all the applause. This is a bit of a stretch, I think, but the themes of the backstage musical – ambition, self-promotion, the tension between bravado and vulnerability – are packaged as a comment on the struggle all good Americans should be going through to better themselves. The musical in the early days aspired with an almost ideological fervour to the condition of being American. It just so happened that, in 1985, being American was what everyone else wanted to be too.

I recently asked my dad if he'd enjoyed all those shows we went to in the '80s, or if he'd rather have been doing something else, like mowing the lawn or eating stair tacks. He said, 'No, I enjoyed them. Nice music. Easy listening. They were good evenings out.'

'But had you ever been to a musical before you met Ma?'

'Er, no.'

'Why not?'

'Well. They weren't my sort of thing.'

I asked if he remembered *42nd Street*.

'It's one of my favourites actually.'

'Name a tune,' I said suspiciously.

'"Shuffle off to Buffalo". Where the underclass can meet the . . . what was it?' He frowned.

'The elite.'

*

It is ironic that musicals, which urge their audience to be ambitious at every turn, to aim, always, for the big time, should themselves be regarded as such an unambitious art form. Even use of the phrase 'art form' in this context will make some people scoff. Musicals are for people who are too thick for opera and too square for pop music. They are for people from the sticks, who twice yearly put on evening dress and migrate en masse to the major capitals of the world where they enjoy themselves by watching things they have seen before at twice the price they paid last time. Musicals are for the sorts of people who, even though their coach will be waiting outside the theatre after the show, still take their umbrellas.

It wasn't until I moved to London myself that I understood the attitude of Londoners towards people who live out of town. And it wasn't until I was on a trip to New York that I understood how much I had adopted it.

In my mid-twenties I saw an old-fashioned production of *42nd Street* on Broadway. I was with two friends, one a female fan of musicals, the other a 27-year-old man whom we'd surprised with tickets for his birthday. (He was quite surprised.) I hadn't been to a show of this kind for many years, although I'd been to lots of upmarket revivals – the Sam Mendes production of *Cabaret* at the Donmar Warehouse; Richard Eyre's *A Little Night Music* at the National Theatre, featuring Judi Dench's seminal performance of 'Send in the Clowns'. This felt like something of a homecoming.

It was midsummer in New York and the theatre was hot. As we

waited for the overture to begin, I took a look at the people sitting around us. How ludicrously overdressed they are, I thought; and overloud, stuffed into tiny seats in the upper circle so that every time they walked along a row, the chance of a death plunge into the stalls below seemed a real and terrifying possibility. Voluminous women shushed each other's rustling sounds while their menfolk gazed about in vain hope of a bomb scare. 'I can't see the show,' complained the woman to my right, on account of how the woman in front of us had built her hair into an amazing tower block.

'Honey, you wanna swap seats with me?' said her husband.

'I don't think that will help, honey,' she said, and sighed. The female friend I was with took off her shoes and hooked her toes over the back of the seat in front, garnering filthy looks across 360 degrees.

'Pathetic,' I thought.

It was a bad production, with a demoralized cast and limp choreography. Having the actual 42nd Street right outside didn't help matters. It seemed bizarre that people would come on holiday to New York only to pay lots of money to see this phoney version of the city. It confirmed to the man in our party what he had always suspected: that people who like musicals don't do so because musicals are good, but because they appeal to some childish, provincial need in them that serious theatre doesn't fulfil.

'Pathetic,' I thought, and a moment later slammed into myself, coming back the other way.

*

The difference between an interest and a passion is that an interest works on you from the outside in, whereas with a passion it's the other way round. That's why people see their passions reflected in every surface, every circumstance. I loved *42nd Street* because it took me out of myself and made me think there was a bigger and more exciting world out there than could be seen from north Buckinghamshire. But it wasn't much more to me than that.

While most adult musicals bored me, I thought the ones made for children were just the bloody end. The achingly dull *Bedknobs and Broomsticks*; little orphan Annie with her freckles and nauseating false modesty. That scene where she offers to scrub the floors at the Warbucks mansion then uses emotional blackmail to screw extra treats out of the old guy? I wanted to suspend her from a coat hook by the socket of one eye. The only interesting thing about Oliver Twist was that in real life his cousin Linda had worked with my mother in London. The children in *Chitty Chitty Bang Bang* were full of contrived silliness and too cute, like an adult's idea of how an amusing child should be. They were Shirley Temples to Judy Garland's Judy Garland, actual children, that is, as opposed to a seventeen-year-old pretending to be a child, which is why, with her air of mysterious maturity, Dorothy Gale was the only one who had any appeal in the first place.

Lots has been written about the appeal to small girls of another small girl fighting off lions and killing a witch, but it is worth repeating that the useless figures in *The Wizard of Oz* are all men and the powerful ones all women. *The Wizard of Oz* is an adult film in children's clothing. All those threats of torture – the scarecrow being threatened with a match, the witch's promise that the last to go would see the other three go before her – I found it thrilling and horrifying and totally absorbing.

And then, one day, I found a tape down the back of the sideboard. It didn't look like my other tapes, which were Tubby the Tuba, Sparky's Magic Piano and Wendy Craig reading the works of Beatrix Potter. This tape had a glum-looking woman on the front, shrouded in black, who my mother said was the same woman who had played Dorothy in *The Wizard of Oz*. When I played it her voice sounded odd, as if she'd eaten a sandwich and had crumbs still at large in her windpipe. She sang a song called 'You'll Never Walk Alone'. I didn't know it came from a show called *Carousel* and that it was sung, in the original score, by someone called Claramae Turner with Shirley Jones tremulously chipping in as she wept over the body of her good-for-nothing but mercifully dead husband, Billy Bigelow. It's an example of a song that can only be sung in the spirit in which it was written: as if your abusive husband has just been knifed after a foiled robbery and the clams from the lunch table not yet cold.

'Do you remember that sampler you gave me?' says Claramae with nun-like strength and dignity. 'Do you remember what it says?' And while Billy turns blue, Shirley and Claramae duet in staunch forbearance of what it is to be a woman.

We were required, at that time, to eat school lunches and a policy of clean plates was enforced. Failure to eat something resulted in the order to carry your plate to the front, in a dining room walk of shame.

(Our dilemma was the inverse of Oliver Twist's: generally, we wanted less.) If there is an effective way to carry tinned tomatoes on a rimless plate, I don't know what it is. Looking back, what amazes me is that whole tinned tomatoes were served as a vegetable dish in the first place. The tomatoes on my plate were veined and pinkish. When you pushed a fork into their skin they leaked a watery fluid. I had in my head an age – twenty-five – when you could make things happen just by doing them, rather than by studying the way someone else did them and copying it in a slightly shabby and less convincing fashion. I stood there, plate in hand. 'Well?' said the teacher. Well?

The immediate problem was that I had eaten all the food around the tomatoes, so there was no possibility of creating a bulwark against their inevitable journey to the edge of the plate. They trembled and slid to one side. I tilted the plate to absorb them and they slid to the other. Eventually they stabilized and I started to walk, one foot in front of the other, towards the top table. As the scale of my task became clear, the dining room fell quiet. The tomatoes swayed rhythmically, back and forth, in an hypnotic dance that made me think that in all the world there was only me and them, them and me. I dipped my plate at the front and they slid right up to the edge; juice slopped. I stared so hard at their surface that I thought I could see them throbbing.

I got halfway to the front before losing it.

Who knows why or how – it doesn't matter now – but the right hand side of the plate fell below the critical angle and as if in slow motion they belly-flopped onto the wooden floor. The sound they made as they landed was wet and leaden. The crowd gasped. I looked at the teacher.

'Well?' he said. 'Don't just stand there. Pick them up.'

Pick them up. Slowly I got to my hands and knees and crawled under the bench. The dining room erupted in jeers. Like all great torch songs, if you get the sentiment right then it is eminently and endlessly adaptable. As I chased my lunch under the table and mayhem reigned above, it seemed to me that 'You'll Never Walk Alone' meant quite the opposite from what it appeared on the surface to be saying. It meant that in all likelihood you *would* walk alone but that whatever happened in life, you had to pick up your tomatoes and carry on, with hope in your heart. It was the iron in the glove of all great musicals: self-reliance, self-reliance, self-reliance.

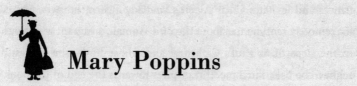

Mary Poppins

What Would Barbra Do?

In the book on which the 1964 film *Mary Poppins* is based, the heroine materializes at number 17 Cherry Tree Lane not by gliding serenely down through the sky, in dignified contrast to all the nannies she has just sent flying, but as a dark shape hurled against the gate by the wind, then picked up again and flung violently at the house.

The original Poppins has small eyes to denote shrewdness. She is very vain, constantly gazing at herself in reflective surfaces and concluding 'very smart, very interesting'. She throws out terrible glances and levitates Uncle Albert's landlady against her will. She is not remotely sentimental about the Bird Woman, a vagrant who clogs up the steps of St Paul's Cathedral and whose birds, she suggests, ought to be baked in a pie. It transpires towards the end of the book that Mary Poppins has a cousin at the zoo, who is a snake. All of which is rather strange, given that Poppins has come to stand for a nauseating kind of niceness. But as it turns out, and as her creator, P. L. Travers, put it, she is a woman who 'never wastes time being nice'.

I first encountered *Poppins* at my friend Gina's house, the kind of house – there is one in every childhood – which makes your own look as if it is still functioning under wartime rationing. Who, in 1983, had dental floss? Or an electric toothbrush? Or a hammock? Long before it was fashionable, eight-year-old Gina declared intolerance to dairy produce and ate her cereal in the morning doused with orange juice. So, in imitation, did I. It tasted foul, but that was the price you paid for life in the avant-garde.

Mary Poppins

Our after-school routine revolved around playing 'Chopsticks' on the piano, playing suicide chess, playing In the Sack, in which one of us climbed into a sack and the other goaded next door's terrier, Ian, into attacking it for ninety seconds – or watching one of Gina's two videos, *The Snowman* and *Mary Poppins*. Since *The Snowman* gets a little mushy after the fiftieth viewing, we watched *Mary Poppins*. We watched *Mary Poppins* twice a week for a period of some three years.

My mother thought *Poppins* was silly, partly, I suspect, because she couldn't forgive Julie Andrews for *The Sound of Music*. The only thing she liked about Mary Poppins was her teeth; if I brushed properly, she said, that's how mine would turn out (she couldn't have known it, but I was sneaking off every five minutes at Gina's house to use the electric toothbrush). She found the music trite and the magic annoying. The whole point of a musical, she thought, was that it *wasn't* supposed to be magic. When people sang to each other or danced on the ceiling you weren't supposed to take it literally; it was a way of illustrating feelings so intense that they couldn't be got at via the usual means. A musical that didn't know this didn't know anything.

We didn't think of *Mary Poppins* as a musical, just as one doesn't think of one's parents as belonging overly to the human race. It was a structural necessity, and as such defied broader categorization. And it wasn't the magic we loved about it. What we loved was that here was an authority beyond the parental, wiser, more powerful and with infinitely better dentistry. Poppins is not afraid to answer back. She always has the last word. When she reads out the children's advertisement for a nanny, the paper she clutches has clearly been torn up and stuck together again. And yet, when Mr Banks starts rooting about in the coals, trying to find the paper he discarded there, Poppins looks appalled and says, 'I beg your pardon, are you ill?' (We took this phrase up and used it widely, irrespective of context, along with 'Close your mouth please, Michael, we are not a cod fish,' and Ellen the maid's line, 'No ma'am, I haven't done me brasses yet.')

The most amazing scene in the film, to us, wasn't the tea party on the ceiling, or the jumping into the chalk pavement picture, it was when Mr Banks attempts to fire Mary Poppins for allowing his children to consort with chimney sweeps. Poppins tells him where to get off in no uncertain terms. 'Let me make one thing *quite* clear,' she snorts. 'I never explain anything.'

'I never explain anything,' I said to my mother after cooking grass cuttings in the oven.

'What did you say?' she said, travelling across the linoleum at the speed of light.

The first Poppins book was written in 1934, but it is set twenty years earlier, at the end of the Edwardian age. Pamela Travers had been in England for ten years by then. Like her heroine she was not, by all accounts, nice: nice in the sense of being altogether acceptable to polite society. She was Australian, for a start, which in 1924 would have guaranteed that a certain amount of condescension came her way. And she had come from a rather bleak and chaotic background in provincial Queensland. Born Helen Goff, Travers was the product of an alcoholic, bank manager father, who died when she was seven, and a mother whose method of coping alone with three children was, on at least one occasion, to run from the house threatening suicide.

As soon as she was old enough, Goff changed her name – Travers was her father's Christian name, so she must have retained some warm memories of him – and came to England where she set up as a vivacious and ambitious journalist, freelancing for, among others, the *Sun*. She was thirty-three when she wrote *Mary Poppins*, her first book, and there would be ten more in the series, the last of which was written eight years before she died, in 1988.

Poppins appears on the Banks family doorstep with no announcement and no apparent history, rather as Travers rocked up in London in the 1920s. Her tone in the book has an unusual bite. Poppins is full of observations about the British class system that are equally mocking and approving. Mrs Banks is lightly sent up for competing with the neighbours, but Poppins is admiringly portrayed as a snob; she talks about 'the best people' and is appalled when the butcher tries to chat her up. And yet she is surprisingly placeable in the class system, towards the lower end as Travers would have seen it, rough and ready and not at all prissy. She says unladylike things such as 'strike me pink!' and calls the birds, in the accent that proved so beyond Dick Van Dyke, 'sparrers'.

Although the book is set in the Edwardian age, it is very modern; there are all sorts of episodes in which it kicks against convention. In the story 'Miss Lark's Andrew', Travers writes of the occupants of the house next door, a batty old spinster and her pedigree dog, Andrew. Andrew is a toy breed who goes to the hairdresser twice a week and dines on oysters. He wishes he could be 'common' like his 'special friend', Willoughby, a half Airedale, half retriever. Willoughby is a rough old sort who is always in trouble. Andrew wants Willoughby to move in with them, but Miss Lark refuses. She calls Willoughby a 'great hulking mongrel'. And so Andrew runs away and Miss Lark's heart is broken. Eventually, rather than lose Andrew, she is forced to accept their crossbreed, same-sex relationship. For 1934, I call this progressive.

One of the key mysteries of the film is how the Bankses can afford to live in such splendour on a middle-manager's salary. The answer lies in the book; they can't. Number 17 Cherry Tree Lane is the shabbiest in the street and the family is under constant threat of financial collapse. In the opening scene Mr Banks is grumbling about the cost of his household and his wife, in a very modern equation, is presented with the choice of having four children and being skint or having fewer children and a ritzier lifestyle. She chooses the latter – Jane and Michael's baby twin siblings, John and Barbara, were excised from the film.

There are big, metaphysical plates underpinning *Poppins* the book, which might explain why it found such favour with the likes of T. S. Eliot and Sylvia Plath. Compare the moral universe that Jane and Michael Banks inhabit to the one created by Enid Blyton, who was publishing around the same time, and whose habit it was to give her children unpleasant characteristics and then have them suffer horrible mishaps, to teach their young readers a lesson. Travers was much more subtle than this. Her heroine harbours the very la-di-da opinion that we exist most fully as figments of each other's imaginations. It is why she is forever looking in mirrors: to convince herself that she does, actually, exist. After every adventure, Poppins denies that anything out of the ordinary has happened and the children are forced to ask themselves serious questions about the nature of reality; they learn about perspective and the value of not always believing what they see. Nothing has intrinsic value, implies Poppins, only symbolic. At the end of one story Mrs Corry, the despotic sweet shop owner, climbs a ladder to hang stars in the sky. Jane looks on and asks, 'Are the stars gold paper or is the gold paper stars?'

There are sorrows of a very adult kind lurking in the book, and terrors, too: disaster is only averted by the heroine's ability to control her environment at all times, which you can read as Travers's rebuke to her own messy childhood. There is a trip to the zoo in the middle of the night in which the children find monkeys riding the back of an old man and Admiral Boom, who failed to leave before closing time, imprisoned in a cage, and a seal who asks bitterly of the children how they would like to dive for orange peel. This isn't the usual pantomime villainy, but surreal, disturbing, anarchic, grotesque – the work of a very adult imagination. The snake who is Mary Poppins's cousin kisses her on each cheek and regards the children not entirely benignly. The reason for the midnight gathering is Poppins's birthday, which the author explains is the one night of the year when ancient grievances are shelved and natural predators dance with their prey. The snake gives her his shed skin as a present and then delivers a speech in which he suggests that to eat and to be eaten amount to much the same thing, when we are as 'one, moving to the same end'. It is an extraordinary piece of atheism for a children's book, the conclusion of which, underlined by the nanny's abrupt departure, is that we are all, at some stage, going to die.

In the story 'Christmas Shopping', Maia, a star in human form, comes down from the heavens to buy Christmas presents for her family. She walks through a department store practically naked, draped in a bit of sky, and people huff and puff and threaten to write to *The Times* about it. Blyton would doubtless have had Maia impaled on a railing for her insolence, but Travers, in a rare show of sentiment, uses Maia to make a point about kindness. Despite being short of cash, Mary Poppins gives Maia her own gloves to keep the child warm. As she prepares to leave Maia says, 'I've been so happy,' and it sounds as mournful as a Victorian death scene. Unthinkably, Mary Poppins gets tears in her eyes.

After a year of repeat viewing, we knew the script by heart. We thought of *Mary Poppins* as a secret language only we understood; we didn't know that it was written by the Sherman brothers in cod-Edwardian English and that no one understood it. Have you ever *listened* to the lyrics? They could've been written by Thomas Carlyle.

Richard M. Sherman and his brother, Robert B., were staff writers at Disney who before *Poppins* landed on their desks had written the music for lots of made-for-TV films with titles such as *Escapade in Florence* and *Miracle of the White Stallions*. After its success, they went on to do *Bedknobs and Broomsticks*, *The Aristocats*, *Chitty Chitty Bang*

Bang and most of the songs, including 'I Wanna Be Like You', in *The Jungle Book*. They tried to repeat the *Poppins* formula in the 1976 musical *The Slipper and the Rose*, with Richard Chamberlain as Prince Charming to Gemma Craven's Cinderella. Where the verbosity in *Poppins* is tightly controlled, *The Slipper and the Rose* is just gibberish.

The beauty of the *Poppins* script is its combination of long strings of incomprehensible words with short, sharp ones. You'll get a windy speech by Mr Banks on the meaning of Englishness, followed by a few abrupt lines by Poppins and some blather from Bert. Despite his ridiculousness, Bert delivers the most magical line of the film, during the scene around the fireplace when he peers up through the soot to the night sky and speaks wonderingly of the world when it is halfway in shadow and halfway in light. On the rooftops of London, he says, 'Coo, what a sight.' It turns out that, of all the adventures they go on, the most extraordinary thing is seeing the London skyline at dusk.

The *Poppins* script became so ingrained in our minds that we developed a game, based on top trumps, in which lines from the film were graded according to difficulty and traded at high speed. For example, the line 'heirs to my dominion', from Mr Banks's opening song, might be countered with 'snuffed aborning', from his soliloquy at the end. We didn't know what a dominion was or why it was airy, which meant that the game was not only a test of memory but also of intuition, of judging the difficulty of one incomprehensible phrase relative to another. The scoring was haphazard and as the game went on it became necessary to enforce, sometimes physically, the rule against fudging or mumbling. 'Shipyards, the mercantile!' signalled the start. It is sung by Mr Dawes Snr, the head of the bank, whilst lecturing young Michael on where to invest his tuppence.

'Shipyards, the mercantile!' said Gina.

'View halloo,' I said. This is cried by the cartoon huntsman as he chases Mary Poppins on her runaway carousel horse.

'Oh, yes, view halloo.' This is said by the fox as it jumps aboard the horse to escape the hunt.

'You can't have that.'

'The fox says it.'

'I said it first.'

'It's different.'

'You can't have it.'

'Edifice.' A good, solid play. It occurs during Mr Banks's superlatively acted breakdown, the heart of the film, when David Tomlinson portrays with agonizing tenderness the plight of a man who has been fired, whose children have run away, who sees all that he holds dear crumbling around him, who has failed, as he says in a phrase worth ten points if I could only have dredged it up in its entirety, 'to carve his niche in the edifice of time'. (Tomlinson pronounces 'niche' in this sentence to rhyme with 'stitch' not 'quiche', adding brilliantly to his air of uptightness.) He was a fine actor, Tomlinson, a former Grenadier Guard who had served as a flight lieutenant during the war.

'Majestic, self-atomizing canals.' This occurs during Dawes Snr's speech in the bank, but since we never knew what 'self-atomizing' was (or indeed 'self-amortizing' as it turns out to be, which means 'to write off an expenditure for, by prorating over a certain period') it always caused problems.

'Majestic what?'

'Self-amatizing. Appetizing. Canals.'

'Cheat.'

You could either carry on at this stage or grab a handful of school jumper and rotate in a malevolent square dance, trying to land kicks while keeping your own shins out of range.

'Think of the foreclosures.'

'Fraught with purpose.'

'Impertinent suggestion.'

'Noblesse oblige.'

'Highly questionable outings of every other kind.'

'Fiduciary duty.' Top trump.

Damn.

I would keep 'forbearance is the hallmark of your creed' up my sleeve for when I was in a tight corner. It had magnificence to it, like an artichoke on a bed of lettuce.

The end of the game was signalled by use of our favourite line, 'Take heart for Mrs Pankhurst has been clapped in irons again!' Mrs Banks sings it when she sweeps through the house in the opening scene after marching with the suffragettes. We thought Mrs Pankhurst was a made up person, like Mrs Mop. 'Pankhurst' was clearly one of the funniest words ever invented.

*

In some ways more interesting than Mary Poppins herself is her alter ego, the Bird Woman, who sits on the steps of St Paul's Cathedral repeating her one line of the film: 'Feed the birds. Tuppence a bag.' We spent a lot of time thinking about the Bird Woman. She had no magical powers and so, unlike Poppins, was subject to the traditional relationship between cause and effect. We wondered about her background. What had happened to her family? Where did she go at night?

The Bird Woman gives an impression of fatness, her bulk spilling over a waist drawn in with a bit of string, but the likelihood is that she is wearing every scrap of clothing she owns and that underneath she is quite thin. Her expression is serene and her hair appears as little wisps of cotton wool and she is wearing a hat, which implies that despite her wretched circumstances she still takes pride in her appearance. When she coos at the pigeons in a low, flat voice, it is clear that they mean more to her than a source of income. We were frightened by her poverty and by her serenity in the face of it, which was eerier than if had she been grim-faced and miserable.

The Bird Woman is a mythical figure in *Poppins*. It is she who triggers the chain of events that results in Mr Banks losing his job. She makes only a fleeting appearance in the book, but in the film, when Michael refuses to invest his tuppence at the bank in preference to feeding the birds, she serves to illustrate a point about social responsibility, one that the author would, as she did with so much of the film, doubtless have found crass and sentimental. One imagines

Travers siding with Dawes Snr, the head of the bank, on the issue of avian welfare in the capital. What, asks Mr Dawes of Michael, does one get in return for feeding the birds? Fat birds.

The fact that Poppins chooses to sing a song about her gives the Bird Woman a symbolic weight disproportionate to her short amount of screen time. In 'Feed the Birds', which Poppins sings to the children in the nursery one evening, she describes the 'little old bird woman' carrying a bag of crumbs to feed the 'little birds', and calling to them, an Edwardian bird-whisperer, in her own 'special way'. The birds appear in the film as white cartoon doves, but it is useful to remind ourselves that it's pigeons we're talking about here, clearly not a species the American songwriters had any experience of. The song goes on to speculate that 'although you can't see it' you know 'they are smiling' each time someone 'shows that he cares'. It's not clear whether it's the pigeons who are smiling or the 'saints and apostles' who adorn the upper reaches of the cathedral and look protectively down on the Bird Woman, a religious flourish that led us, in later years, to speculate that a Christian allegory could be mapped onto the entire film: after morally repositioning the Banks family, Poppins disappears into the sky, never to be seen again. At a certain drunken point in the evening, this becomes an obvious nod by Disney to the ascension.

If Travers ever gave any thought to the film's sanctification of the birds, it might have pleased her to note that a smiling pigeon is in all likelihood a pigeon that has just shat on your head. We didn't care about the birds, hungry or otherwise. It was the Bird Woman, sitting on the cold pavement, calling out to punters in a cracked voice, that seemed more dramatic and pitiful to us than anything we'd yet come across in life.

It wasn't until years later that I discovered from a TV documentary that the Bird Woman was played by an actress called Jane Darwell, who was eighty-five at the time and something of a Hollywood legend. Her career as an actress went back to the silent movie era, when she made a lot of cowboy films, such as *War of the Cattle Range* and *The White Squaw*. Growing up on a ranch in Missouri, she had wanted to be a fat lady in the circus and then an opera singer, but had settled eventually for acting and made her first film in 1913, a silent western called *The Capture of Aguinaldo*. By the 1930s she was already playing grandmothers and aged aunts. She played Mrs Dolly Merriwether in *Gone With the Wind* in 1939, and her finest dramatic role came a year later, when she played Ma Joad in John Ford's film of the Steinbeck novel *The Grapes of Wrath*, for which she won an Oscar.

Darwell was living in a retirement home for actors in California when Walt Disney approached her to play the Bird Woman. She turned the offer down, so Disney came personally to visit and eventually she consented. I like to think that you can hear the experience of a hundred and fifty films in that one line of hers. She died of a heart attack three years after the film came out, aged eighty-eight.

I can remember the exact moment at which it became clear that our relationship with *Poppins* was going to have to end, or, at least, to modify. It came one Saturday morning out of the blue when Gina said, 'I fancy Morten Harket.' Morten Harket: the words made me think of a sandy-coloured creature with little ears and talons.

'Me too,' I said.

She looked at me slyly. 'Who is he?' she said.

'I don't have to tell you.'

This was before the under-tens were required to hold a position on pop music. Even at thirteen you could hold off enquiries by mumbling Radio 1. But at nine years old it was still admissible to have no idea who was in the charts or even what the charts were.

A poster of Morten Harket and the rest of his band, A-Ha, materialized in her bedroom, which to make things more interesting she stuck to the inside face of an exposed structural beam. To see it you had to climb on top of the wardrobe. 'Let's play Morten Harket' meant one person sitting on the wardrobe while the other person played A-Ha's 1984 chart hit 'The Sun Always Shines on TV' on the tape deck below. After a few weeks we forgot about A-Ha and went back to *Poppins*. Life continued. And then one day we were sitting in the living room watching the video when Gina's older sister, Martha, came in with her friend Chloe, who lived up the road. Chloe liked to begin her sentences with 'For your information'.

'Can we go to the shops now?'

'For your information, no.'

They slumped into the beanbags and stared derisively at the screen.

'"Papa Don't Preach" is about being pregnant,' said Chloe

suddenly. She started to sing about how she'd made up her mind and was keeping her baby.

'What do *you* think?' she said, looking at me with beady, bird-like eyes, the sort of bird that might peck you to death.

I stared at the floor, which was brown with bits of disengaged thread where the cat had scratched it.

Chloe snorted. 'What's wrong with you? Are you a herman?'

I've thought about this from time to time since then, and I think what she must have meant was 'Are you a hermit', confusing the word 'herman' for the word 'hermit' and the word 'hermit' for the word 'mute'. 'Are you a mute?' is what she was aiming for, I think, unless it was 'Are you a German?', but this was before any of us had an idea of what a German was, i.e. pre the German school exchange, after which 'Are you a German?' gained currency as an insult.

'No,' I said, reflexively.

'Are you a virgin?' she said.

'No,' I said.

She started to sing, 'You're not a virgin, you're not a virgin,' and then, 'Like a virgin, touched for the very first time.'

Me and Gina looked at each other.

Gina stuck out her chin. 'Go away,' she said.

'Go away, go away,' mocked Chloe. She smirked and straightened up. 'For your information,' she said, 'Madonna and Sean Penn are getting divorced,' and with that she got up off the beanbag and the two of them flounced out of the room. We went back to watching *Poppins* and would continue to do so for a while afterwards, but something had been spoilt. Before we reached our eleventh birthdays, it started to feel childish and backward and embarrassingly far removed from whatever Madonna and Sean Penn, whoever they might be, were doing. And then Gina and I were put in different classes at school and stopped hanging out and that was the end of that.

P. L. Travers was largely horrified by what Disney had done to her book. She thought it conservative and silly and unsubtle. *Mary Poppins* was made in 1964, early enough in the decade for it to still espouse 1950s values, and it has been said that Mrs Banks's flighty approach to women's suffrage was designed to ridicule equally flighty notions women in the '60s were getting about liberation.

I hadn't seen *Mary Poppins* for years when it came on TV last Christmas. I wondered how much I would remember – all of it, as it turned out, right down to self-amortizing canals. I was surprised by how good it was and also, contrary to Travers's view, how subtle. It seemed to me that Mrs Banks, while being dizzy and ridiculous, was also capable of giving her husband some very cool and appraising looks that were clearly intended to humour him until he came to his senses. When she said, 'Oh, George, how clever of you!' it served only to emphasize his idiocy. The way she was militant out of the home and meek within it showed up failures in the women's movement and Poppins herself was an irrefutable feminist.

Travers abhorred the transformation of Mrs Banks into a suffragette even more than she hated the cartoon penguins, and considered it a liberty the story didn't support. She thought the film had turned Mr Banks into a petty tyrant and not the benign father she had envisaged. She harangued Walt Disney himself at the premiere but he gave her a withering look and said it was too late. The film won five Oscars, but Travers remained ambivalent about it. She would probably have preferred the current West End stage show, in which Mrs Banks is a housewife without a cause and the children are terrorized by puppets in the nursery.

This was in some ways an unlikely Disney film. Although Mr Banks is, in the best Hollywood tradition, a man who has forgotten how to dream, his emotional journey is saved from sentimentality by the sheer force of David Tomlinson's performance. Gina and I were astonished to see the dad of the family almost crying in his breakdown scene, so frustrated is he by his own lack of progress. When he is humiliated at the bank – 'No! not that!' cries one of the partners as Dawes Jnr prepares to punch a hole in his bowler hat – it seemed to us to do terrible violence to the notion of parental infallibility. He was weak and a bit silly, sillier than Mrs Banks, who at least in quieter moments was shown to have self-awareness. And although they got together in the end, in the usual Disney way, the Bankses were equal in their ineptitude as parents and equally culpable for failures within the family.

Predictably, Mary Poppins's departure in the book is signalled by a 'wild cry' from the wind, which violently displaces her from the doorstep. The end of the film is supposed to be happy but it didn't strike me as happy at all. It wasn't sad like when the fox dies at the end of *The Fox and the Hounds*, or when King Kong peels off the side of the Empire State building (naturally I had seen the 1933 version with Fay Wray and cried so hard at the end of it that my mother, hearing me from the garden, thought someone had broken into the house and was murdering me). It seemed crueller than both of these, because you were expected to feel good about it.

At the end of *Mary Poppins*, the nuclear family triumphs and Mr Banks gets his job back, Dawes Snr having 'died laughing' when the penny finally dropped on the joke Banks told him about the man with the wooden leg named Smith. Mrs Banks becomes more directly involved in the lives of her children and in the final scene, the Bankses fly their kites in a triumphant show of family unity over the short-term thrill of a supernatural nanny. But for goodness' sake, what happened when the children got home and discovered she had gone? It was clear to us that a great sacrifice had taken place there on the doorstep. Looking wistfully at her charges, who seem, in a fit of amnesia to have forgotten her already, Poppins sighs and concludes, 'It is as it should be,' resigning herself to a life in which her only constant companion is a talking umbrella handle.

We found the display of family unity in the final scenes unconvincing. The Bankses are reconciled, but would Mr Banks ever really understand his wife's commitment to women's suffrage? Had Mrs Banks even asked her husband what happened that terrible night at the bank?

And while in hopeful mood we would speculate on the likelihood of Poppins and Bert's getting together at some point in the future, the fact is, come the closing credits, she is off into the sky and that's the end of that. 'Don't stay awai too long,' says Bert wistfully, lifting his cap, and Poppins smiles down at him in a fond, pitying kind of way that seems to say, 'Really, Bert, I don't have the requisite vulnerabilities for marriage. Don't you know that by now?'

Men Who Hate Musicals

What Would Barbra Do?

When I was twelve years old my friend Sophie and I became briefly obsessed with a made-for-TV movie about a little girl called Carrie-Lou. I don't remember the name of the film, or anything much about it beyond the tragic circumstances that led to Carrie-Lou's downfall. She was poor, small and wore glasses; she didn't have a father; she was the target of vicious neighbourhood bullies. One day, in an effort to escape her tormentors, she ran onto the railway track where her fear and shortsightedness combined to blind her to the sight of the oncoming freight train. The last frame of the movie was a close up of her cracked glasses, lying in the weeds by the railway track, while her mother's voice called faintly in the distance, 'Carrie-Lou! Carrie-Lou! Where are you, Carrie-Lou?'

'Carrie-Lou!' cried Sophie across the classroom, 'where are you, Carrie-Lou?' while I shook my head and replied, 'Her little cracked glasses.'

Some years ago while on holiday in New York, I had a row with my friend Dave that unexpectedly made me think of Carrie-Lou. It was a big row, during the course of which he called me a snob and I called him an inverse snob and he said I had no taste and I said he had no class and the result was that Dave and I sat in different parts of the plane on the way home and still, seven years later, occasionally refer to it, although the exact details of what it was about have become a little vague.

I know what set it off, which was the film *Titanic*. Dave said that it was a really good film; I said that I had enjoyed it but that it was a really bad film; he said if something was enjoyable it couldn't by definition be bad; I said this was ridiculous and that lots of things were enjoyable but bad; he said name one and that is when the thing really took off – I made up the shortfall in facts with hostility. (In the seven intervening years I have come up with a long list of examples starting with Abba and ending with crabsticks.)

As is often the case in heated arguments, you get backed into defending a position more extreme than the one you actually hold. So Dave ended up arguing that *Titanic* was art and I that it was some kind of blasphemy against the twelve hundred souls who went down with the ship. (I regret to say that I probably did use the word 'souls'.) The only bit of the argument I remember with any clarity is the bit involving Billy Zane, in which I said, '*Titanic* can't be art,' and Dave said, 'Why not?' and I said, 'Billy Zane is in it,' and he said, 'I like Billy Zane,' and I said, 'Anything with Billy Zane in it can't, *by definition*, be art,' and he said, 'What if Billy Zane played Hamlet?'

It was unfortunate that we had, that morning, bought tickets for an evening production of *Cats*. They had cost eighty dollars apiece and I had argued against the idea but Dave had insisted because, he said, he had 'heard that it was good'. This exasperated me beyond words. 'What do you mean you've heard it's good? Who from?'

'My nan,' he said and gave me a challenging look.

Sullenly, we left the diner and took a cab to the theatre on 42nd Street. Even the best show in the world can't survive the contorting effect of being watched for use as ammunition in an argument. And this wasn't a good show. In fact, it was terrible. I never saw the appeal of *Cats* in the first place – where's the storyline? – but with an nth generation cast who could barely stay in tune, scabby, threadbare costumes and a half-empty theatre, it was unbearable.

'I suppose you think that's art, too,' I said, afterwards.

I don't know quite what point I'm trying to make here, other than that at the end of its run *Cats* was really bad. I suppose it's that people who hate musicals often think of them as belonging to the *Titanic* and Carrie-Lou end of things, that is to the fun-but-dumb end or the hopelessly melodramatic, and I think of them as belonging somewhere higher up the food chain. When good musicals are silly it is because they intend to be silly, not because, like Zane running around a sinking ship waving a gun, they have aimed for high drama and overshot. And when they are tragic, they are subtler than cracked glasses by the railway line.

At the end of the night, as we sat in a restaurant having another frosty meal, Dave said, 'I don't *really* think *Titanic* is art. I was just winding you up.' Then the meta-argument kicked off about how women argue out of conviction and men out of sport and before you knew it I was in row J and he was in row A and it was all the fault of James Cameron and Andrew Lloyd Webber.

When you break them down into their constituent parts, even the best musicals look ludicrous. The people in them find they can do amazing things, like tease a waltz from a hatstand or dance on the ceiling or build a barn using acrobatics in the place of more traditional construction methods; things that, before they felt a show tune coming on, they simply couldn't do. They go to insane, crackhead lengths to make their point. Take *The Music Man*, a 1962 musical directed by Morton DaCosta and starring Robert Preston and Shirley Jones, in which a con artist blows into town, hastily organizes a children's brass band, then flogs non-existent musical instruments to their parents before shooting through. If more con artists had ambition like this, the world would be a frightening place.

You can imagine the planning meeting:

Producer 1: So this guy goes door-to-door selling cornets . . .
Producer 2: Yeah, and the kids totally buy into it, even the little mute kid who's lost his father . . .
Producer 1: Yeah, because what's been missing all their lives has been –
Producer 2: – brass band music. Except really the guy can't play a note
Producer 1: and nor can the kids, and yet –
Producer 2: – when it comes to the concert
In unison: they find they can play perfectly.

Naturally the con backfires and both the kids and the rogue bandleader learn some tough but valuable lessons about the perils of meddling with community spirit.

Other Musicals Based on Ludicrous Conceits

Follow the Fleet
Director: Mark Sandrich

Starring: Fred Astaire and Ginger Rogers
In which a woman woos a man by restoring her late father's steam ship to working order and offering him its captaincy. (Also in which the line 'Get thee behind me Satan' was censored by the British Film Censors of 1936, but not, interestingly, the line 'A steam schooner? Just the type I like to feel under me. I'd like to be captain of *your* ship.')

Royal Wedding
Director: Stanley Donen
Starring: Fred Astaire and Jane Powell
In which a man woos a woman against the backdrop of an English royal wedding, provoking the native yokels to sing, 'What a lovely day for a wedding / lovely in every way,' counter-provoking other yokels to sing, 'Lovely, lovely, lovely.'

Funny Face
Director: Stanley Donen
Starring: Fred Astaire and Audrey Hepburn
In which a man woos a woman by undermining her theories of French existentialism with the rival philosophy 'Think pink'.

Men Who Hate Musicals

The Pajama Game

Directors: George Abbott and Stanley Donen

Starring: Doris Day and John Raitt

In which a factory superintendent woos the head of the grievance committee by backing her bid for a seven and a half cent pay rise in the face of strong opposition from management.

Carousel

Director: Henry King

Starring: Gordon MacRae and Shirley Jones

In which a man slaps his wife and then falls on his knife and after fifteen years in an antechamber of heaven is given the chance to come back for a day to put things right. But all he ends up doing is slapping his daughter. The star-keeper calls this a 'failure'.

Seven Brides for Seven Brothers

Director: Stanley Donen

Starring: Howard Keel and Jane Powell

In which the women of a nineteenth-century town in Oregon respond to being kidnapped by hillbillies by singing 'Ding dong, ding dong ding, were steeple bells ever quite as gay? Wonderful, wonderful day.'

To get an idea of how musicals must look to unfriendly eyes, you have only to read synopses of the three Rodgers and Hammerstein shows that bombed. Between them the pair won 34 Tony awards,

What Would Barbra Do?

15 Oscars, 2 Pulitzers, 2 Grammys and an Emmy, mostly for their 'golden five' productions – *Oklahoma!*, *South Pacific*, *The King and I*, *Carousel* and *The Sound of Music*. The Rodgers and Hammerstein DVD boxed set throws in *State Fair* as well, one of their earliest collaborations, filmed in 1945 with Dick Haymes and remade in '62 with Pat Boone and, if not exactly a flop, then not a triumph either. The film's only source of suspense derives from speculation over who will win first prize in the fair's mincemeat competition. (I'll save you the bother: it's Mrs Frake.)

As well as these there are three resounding failures in the Rodgers and Hammerstein portfolio, and reading about them you get a sudden sense of how ropy the other six might look to someone coming at them cold, without the benefit of familiarity or an open mind. It's as unsettling as catching sight of a family member unexpectedly in town and watching them for a few moments before making yourself known.

The first Rodgers and Hammerstein flop was *Allegro*, written in 1947 and staged at the Majestic Theatre on Broadway. It was the first time Rodgers and Hammerstein had come up with an original idea for a show and didn't encourage them to repeat the experience. *Allegro* has been called the first ever 'concept' musical – tellingly, seventeen-year-old Stephen Sondheim did work experience on it – and part of the reason it failed was that its pretentious musical structure didn't sit well with its humdrum storyline. It was also quite preachy.

In *Allegro*, an idealistic young man called Joe Jnr decides on a career in medicine and heads off to university, an event marked by the song 'It's a Darn Nice Campus'. After graduating he marries his high school sweetheart, a woman called Jenny, who is ambitious for her young husband and would rather he chucked in medicine, joined her father's business and whisked them away from their small Kansas town to the big city. Jenny is aspirational, but in the wrong way: that is, for material success rather than 'self-fulfilment'. (One is permitted to make money in a musical, but only as a side effect of some nobler cause e.g. pursuing a career in show business.)

Joe Jnr's mother gets wind of her daughter-in-law's plans to leave Kansas and is so shocked and outraged that she dies of a heart attack after singing 'Money Isn't Everything'. Joe Jnr resolves to stick to medicine, but reaches a compromise with his wife by agreeing to transfer to a big city hospital. He and Jenny move to Chicago, where she forces him to throw cocktail parties rather than ministering to the sick. A Greek chorus gives voice to Joe Jnr's anxiety in the song 'Allegro', for which Agnes de Mille provides a ballet sequence, and it's all downhill from there. Joe Jnr's faithful nurse, Emily, can see how miserable his life is making him and to get him back on track sings 'The Gentleman is a Dope'. But Joe Jnr won't listen. It takes a particularly nasty run-in with the hospital's chief physician, Dr Digby Denby, to make him realize how empty his life is. When Joe Jnr discovers that Jenny is having an affair with one of the hospital trustees it's the last straw and he promptly leaves her for Emily, who is good and kind and open to the possibility of a future in the mid-west ('Come Home'). The two move back to Kansas to build a non-profit-making hospital, aided by his father, Joe Snr. Joe Jnr wonders if he has done the right thing, but Joe Snr puts his mind at rest with a great truth: 'Time is like an avalanche; it moves faster than is reasonable.'

Allegro ran for 315 performances at the Majestic, right across the street from *Oklahoma!*, then in its fourth year and still enjoying such packed houses that when a truck strike broke out in New York in 1946, one newspaper columnist wondered sympathetically how Rodgers and Hammerstein were going to get their money to the bank. *Time* magazine called *Allegro* an 'artistic failure' which was 'too big for its boots'. The *New York Times* called it a thing of 'great beauty and purity [which] just missed the final splendor of a perfect work of art'. When a straight play 'just misses' being a 'perfect work of art', it can still be a credible success; but with a musical it is all or nothing. The various elements must be balanced so finely that at no point is the audience able, in an Emperor's New Clothes type flash, to look at the thing and realize how insane it is. A musical has only to be a little bit off for the surface tension to break and the whole thing to collapse, like a soufflé, into awfulness.

In *Pipe Dream* (1955), Rodgers and Hammerstein returned to the old formula of adapting a musical from a successful book, in this case John Steinbeck's *Sweet Thursday*, a racy number set among the down and outs in Cannery Row, the seedy port district of Monterey, California. It involves a biologist called Doc, who hides behind his microscope and writes scientific papers about the life cycle of the squid instead of throwing himself into the romantic fray. The values in his life are all wrong, placing work above love, and the people around him are much the same, part of a diseased generation which has forgotten what matters. In fact, their lives are very much like a lopsided bus, which they lament in the song 'Lopsided Bus'.

It takes the intervention of a determined young homeless woman to make Doc realize that love is more important than success in the field of invertebrate biology. This is Suzy, who after cutting her hand breaking into a bakery introduces herself with the song 'Everybody's Got A Home But Me'. Doc bandages her hand. He shares with her his frustration at being unable to afford the $300 microscope he needs to complete his research. She and his other friends decide to help him out by pulling off a complicated scam which involves auctioning off a building they don't actually own. Suzy meanwhile grows fond of Doc, a fondness she expresses by sneaking into his flat and leaving cakes around the place. He finds this creepy rather than sweet and they have a row, during which Suzy says his big ideas about biology have made him the laughing stock of the neighbourhood. This depresses Doc and he sings 'The Man I Used to Be'. Suzy wonders if she's gone too far and implies in conversation with her friend Fauna that she only lashes out because she has self-esteem issues. Fauna tries to fix these with the song 'Suzy is a Good Thing'. This seems to do the trick and after a walk by the sea, Doc and Suzy get together. Then they split up. Finally, in a brilliant move, Doc's friend Hazel breaks his arm with a baseball bat while he's sleeping, in the hope that this will force Doc to swallow his pride and let Suzy look after him, which it does. All of their friends then ceremonially unveil the gift they have bought for Doc, which is a telescope, not a microscope, but he is so elated by love that he doesn't even care.

Pipe Dream opened at the Shubert Theatre on 30 November 1955 and closed within a year.

The third flop was *Dream of the Rood* the musical, based on the first-century early English poem in which the story of the crucifixion is told from the point of view of the cross. Written in alliterative verse, the ancient text is reworked to incorporate a McCarthyite theme, with Jesus as a Communist and a chorus of gospel singers representing the House Committee on UnAmerican Activities. It took place on a huge stage version of Gethsemane and opened with Joseph planing wood in his workshop, singing, 'Buzz buzz / zoom zoom / I'm in my carpentry commune.' The cross itself had two numbers, 'Wondrous King!' and 'The Burden I Bear' and attracted comparisons in the *New York Times* to the early mystery plays.

Actually, *Dream of the Rood* wasn't written by Rodgers and Hammerstein but by a friend and me in college, our first and last attempt; we got as far as casting Woody Allen as Jesus and lost interest. It doesn't look any more ludicrous on paper, however, than the other two flops, *Flower Drum Song*, a complicated tale of arranged marriage set in San Francisco's Chinatown, and *Me and Juliet*, a musical comedy set backstage at a theatre featuring a man named Charlie and his romantic tribulations with a woman named Lilly. Comic interludes are provided by two electricians called Sidney and Bob and the numbers include 'A Very Special Day', 'That's The Way It Happens' and 'Keep It Gay'.

Occasionally, amateur theatre companies revive these productions as rare, 'lost' musicals, but the truth is most of them deserve to have lapsed into obscurity. Even when the songs were up to scratch, the storylines were so far-fetched they exhausted the audience's credulity. Rodgers and Hammerstein were at their best when they were driving either an historical epic or a sweeping great tragedy; light romantic comedy just flummoxed them.

It's funny. When people don't like metal or jazz or pop or classical music, or when they don't like Westerns or SF movies, they are content, generally, to confine their dislike to avoiding them. When people don't like musicals they feel a need not only to tell you about it, but to convince you of why you shouldn't like them either. The look they get on their faces is similar to the one you see on religious people when they're talking about gangsta rap. It's funny.

It is mostly, although not exclusively, youngish men who take this position, and when asked what it is, exactly, they object to, they talk about lack of realism or sentimentality or the failure of musicals to present anything but the most reactionary view of the world. Sometimes they can't even articulate what it is they don't like.

'Oh really?' said a male friend of mine politely when I told him I was writing this book. 'Musicals like what, *My Fair Lady*?'

'Yep.'

'*Singin' in the Rain*?'

'Yep.'

'*Guys and Dolls*?'

'Yep.'

A pause.

'*Yentl*?'

'Yep.'

And holding up his hands like Dracula caught in a shaft of sunlight, he gave a high-pitched cry and slumped over the table.

The thing is you *could* construct a moral case against musicals – their sexual and racial politics aren't always too hot – but it requires a depth of knowledge that casual musicals-haters just don't have. Their hatred, it seems to me, is mainly conceptual, intuited rather than specified and underpinned, I tend to think, by the presumption of crapness that attends most things valued primarily by women. Freud called it the 'self-indulgent fact-blind ascendancy of the matriarchy', but I prefer Mr Banks's summary in *Mary Poppins*: 'Slipshod, sugary female thinking.'

Forced to put an image to their dislike, the average musicals-hater will go first to the works of the golden age, summoning from some long-ago sitting the memory of red-haired siblings dancing on a plank or women singing to lambs in a barnyard. Musicals of the golden age are those made between 1950 and 1965, when over a third of all films that came out of Hollywood contained singing. In golden age musicals the conceits are more ludicrous, the excesses sillier, the costumes flouncier, the politics more reactionary and the lyrics sappier than anything that came before or after. They are more vulnerable to accusations of nostalgia, gender stereotyping and the falsification of human experience than even the silliest TV sitcoms of the era. In golden age musicals the romantic clichés of spring, June, blossom, nightingales, stars, barnyards and eyes are joined by a whole new set of clichés; bare-chested sailors dance on rooftops and women lean against door jambs, stirring cake mix. People in love are framed in windows. People incapable of love fall on their own knives. The fine liberal sentiments of *South Pacific*, in which an American man falls in love with a Polynesian woman, are undermined by the depiction of Bali-Ha'i natives running around with bones through their noses. The fine, liberal sentiments of *The King and I*, in which Deborah Kerr and Yul Brynner fall in love across the racial divide, are undermined by the casting of Terry Saunders (an American) as Lady Thiang, Yul Brynner (half Russian, half Mongolian) as the King, Rita Moreno (Puerto Rican) as the slave Tuptim and Carlos Rivas as her boyfriend Lun Tha, who seems to have come to Thailand via Romania and the Welsh borders. This is in keeping with the Hollywood principle They All Look The Same. Only Deborah Kerr has any authenticity; she is Scottish, but comes across in the film as English as a cold shower on an icy morning in an unheated house with no windows.

And while they are so thematically and visually repetitive, in the golden age musical there is an eccentric failure to enforce any uniformity of singing style: so, in *South Pacific*, Rossano Brazzi is allowed to roll his Rs and pretend he's doing *Turandot* (in Brazzi's hands, 'Some Enchanted Evening' comes out like 'Nessun Dorma'), while Mitzi Gaynor shakes out jolly pop renditions from a different musical tradition entirely. In *An American in Paris*, Gene Kelly bops about to light jazz while Georges Guétary seems to think he's starring in turn of the century French music hall.

In days gone by, one might have argued that part of the reason why so many men hated musicals is that they were worried that liking them would make them look gay. It is an issue that the musical itself has some hang-ups about. In *South Pacific*, love has so emasculated Rossano Brazzi that he turns down the chance to fight the Japanese and Captain Brackett has to have a stern word with him. Poor show! Doesn't he realize there's something larger at stake here? Like world fucking freedom? But then, as has been established, this is a man who reads Proust. (There is a chippy, anti-intellectual strain running through some musicals, a response to the condescension they suffer at the hands of high art.)

In these metrosexual times however this surely can't be the case. The nature of men's dislike for musicals is so primordial, so resistant to social change and the merits of individual shows that it can only have to do with one thing: their mothers.

The same friend who started frothing at the mouth at the mention of *Yentl* – the very fact he knew what *Yentl* was shows you how progressive he is – told me in vivid detail about the first time he was exposed to a musical, at a retrospective screening of *South Pacific* at his local cinema in the early 1980s.

'Really, dear,' Brian's mother reassured him, as they queued for tickets, 'it's about war.' Little Brian studied the poster and was not reassured: it featured a woman on a beach with flowers round her neck and a man gazing up at her in a way that didn't, to Brian's mind, present as altogether martial. Still, at seven years old he took his mother's word for things and, clutching her hand, he plunged from the heat of the afternoon into the cool, dark foyer of the cinema. (I am recreating this on the basis that all childhood memories before a certain age take place in long, hot summers.)

As the film began, Brian started to relax. There on the screen was Rossano Brazzi, built like a war hero, dressed like a war hero and surrounded by all the exhilarating paraphernalia of World War Two. Bare-chested sailors ran across a beach. A military plane flew across the sky. The war hero looked out over the bay and an expression crept across his face that Brian couldn't quite read. Sort of strained. He looked as if he would like to say something but couldn't quite find the words. He was probably, Brian thought, reliving the time he killed a man. The war hero's face hardened and then he opened his mouth and out came a sound that, at first, Brian couldn't quite place. Hey; wasn't that . . . *singing*?

Brian twisted his neck to look at the people around him. Nobody else seemed to have noticed. The man was singing. Into the face of the woman, who had materialized behind him and had an expression on *her* face that suggested that she, too, might be about to . . . yup, there she went. What *was* this? Wasn't it rude to sing into someone's face like that? Wasn't it embarrassing? Was this his induction into some previously unknown and horrifying facet of adult behaviour?

Brian turned to his mother for reassurance and almost screamed. Her head lolled to one side, her eyes were glazed and teary. She was smiling to herself and her lips were moving slightly. Half an hour later another war hero was singing into the face of another girl – something about touching her hand while his arms grew strong, like a pair of birds that burst with song. Brian didn't even try to work out how arms can burst with song. All he knew was that the sailors on the beach weren't any kind of sailors he wanted to be.

Twenty years on he still shudders at the memory of that first, stinging piece of maternal treachery. 'A war film!'

What freaked out little Brian, apart from the singing, was that whatever was going on between his mother and *South Pacific*, it didn't include him. Just as every woman has a story about the first time she saw *The Sound of Music*, so every man seems to have one about the first time he was force-fed a musical only to discover that while his participation had seemed vital at the outset – a litmus test for his sensitivity or modernity or commitment to the relationship – when it actually came down to it, he was surplus to requirement. (Testimony from my male friends suggests that there are particularly painful memory clusters surrounding their forced-exposure to the shows of the pre-1970s, when the costumes were bigger and the lyrics more inclined towards use of such expressions as 'coo-cooing' and 'mighty glad'.) If he hated the thing he was a sexist fink; if he loved it he was trying to suck up. He couldn't possibly hope to understand the interplay between fantasy, parody and the projection of self-image that was going on between the woman he was with and the action on screen.

By the time my friend Bill was introduced to musicals he was a fully fledged adult and thought he had pretty much mapped out those areas of life that he wanted to avoid. Poor Bill. The response of the average straight man to musical film and theatre is typified by what happened to him one night at the Palace Theatre in Manchester. For reasons unknown, when Bill was a young reporter at the *Irish Times* he was given, along with his regular duties, a special patch to cover: musicals, new ones, the reviewing thereof.

'It's a tough beat, kid, but someone's gotta do it.'

Bill had never seen a musical before. His mother was an opera singer and musicals were looked down on in his house as an inferior art form. Still, being young and naive, he gamely accepted a commission to fly from Dublin to Manchester for the opening night of *Miss Saigon*. He saw it as his first jolly and looked forward, with tragic optimism, to mining it as a rich and rewarding new seam in his career.

'How little I knew,' he says fifteen years on, shaking his head and staring into his whisky and ice.

Superficially, *Miss Saigon* is a man's musical. Set in the Vietnam War, it has lots of butch stage mechanics and the appearance of a helicopter in the finale. These days, a stage musical is nothing without a monstrous special effect descending in the final scene (I'm thinking particularly of the pink snail in *Doctor Dolittle*, Dominion Theatre, 1998, which combined the talents of Philip Schofield as Dolittle and Julie Andrews as the talking parrot). But in 1989, it was still a big deal to leave nothing to the imagination of the audience.

For a while, the unwitting Bill was amply satisfied with the explosions and the flashing lights. But slowly the wistful tone of the music and the inspirational bent of the lyrics started to work on his nerves. The leading lady had a 'heart like the sea' and confessed that 'a million dreams are in me'. The leading man wondered 'how in the light of one night did we come so far?' A good musical wears its moral on its sleeve; a bad one allows it to poke through the surface like a bone through skin after a nasty break. Bill squirmed at the sentiments being played out before him. Did they think that by throwing guns and ammo into the mix it would somehow make the thing cool? By the time the song 'Why God why?' came round, the musical had done its job and Bill was convinced the production was speaking directly to him. 'Lives will change when tomorrow comes,' sang the hero. Too right, thought Bill. In the lavatory at half time he sat smoking a spliff. 'But even that didn't work,' he says miserably. 'God, this thing just went on and on. I thought it would never end.'

You can divide the elements of the musical that men find most troubling roughly into three: the singing, the action and the moral dimension. Let's start with the singing.

It's not the singing per se that's the problem, but the transition from the talking to the singing. At least in opera – and this argument is usually furthered by people who would rather swallow a razor blade than sit through *Aida* – you don't notice how silly the set-up is because its silliness is consistent; when people communicate through song alone, it is easier to believe them than when they try to get by using an unstable combination of talking, singing and barn-dancing.

In the early days musicals got round the problem of realism by permitting songs to appear only in the context of a show within the show. The lone figure on stage is the most powerful image the musical has, a metropolitan equivalent to the pioneer, peering through the footlights into darkness and reminding the audience of its country's founding principles: that getting ahead is not a practical but a spiritual necessity; that self-promotion serves the public good.

Then in the late 1920s the 'integrated' musical evolved, in which songs occurred as a substitute for speech and, rather than acting as a break in the narrative, moved the action along. As Brian discovered, you could usually see the song coming a mile off, like the look on a child's face between their falling and screaming: a sort of wild-eyed outrage as the pressure rises beneath the surface in search of an outlet.

The musical's unreliable symbolic order is problematic, but there is a certain logic to it. A character only sings when he or she is so profoundly moved, either by joy or misery, that speech is no longer adequate – just as Shakespeare moves between poetry and prose for the same reasons. It's a metaphor, the way David Banner turning into the Incredible Hulk is a metaphor for anger. Nobody complains about that, or about kung fu or zombie films being unrealistic, and the musical makes as much sense within the bounds of its own conventions as they do. It is said that musicals combine realism with fantasy in a way that doesn't hold together. But they *aren't* realistic, not the script nor the art direction nor the action, all of which are made as unrealistic as possible, to allow the leap from speech to song to seem less jarring.

The Action

The action in a musical is supposed to be unreal and dream-like, like the unreal and dream-like nature of one's interior life; it's not like the characters in a Ken Loach flick suddenly bursting into song or dancing on the ceiling. There's a consistency of tone in a musical which means that, even when it gets the budget to shoot on location, the director will often take the edge off the realism by putting a yellow filter over the camera or having the characters speak in a way that isn't quite naturalistic. You might have mistaken it for bad acting, but it's supposed to be like that, sort of dopey, like the Tin Man in *The Wizard of Oz*, or clipped and cryptic, like Rossano Brazzi in *South Pacific*.

Everything is compressed, as in a fable or a poem, and courtship takes place in a matter of minutes. Apart from anything else who wants to hang around until the second half for a love song? The quickest courtship of any I've seen occurs in *South Pacific*, when Joe Cable woos Liat, the daughter of Bloody Mary, in approximately twelve seconds. 'Hello,' he says and gets straight to the point: 'Are you afraid of me?' (This is a popular chat-up line; Billy Bigelow says it to Julie Jordan in *Carousel* and Pat Gilbert to Margy Frake in *State Fair*. It's supposed to imply flashy over-confidence in the man and, when she stands up to him, equal spunkiness in the woman.) Liat, who thankfully can't speak English and slow the thing down, doesn't answer but looks at Joe with big, mournful eyes in which are reflected all the troubles of the world and then they kiss. The kiss is no ordinary kiss; the neck undulates like a charmed snake while the lips press shut and the mouth strains and puckers as if trying to suck concrete mix through a straw. It's an attempt to show passion without attracting the attention of the 1958 censors. Joe and Liat kiss, and the next thing you know they're frolicking in a waterfall and he has given her his father's pocket watch.

The more patient shows buy time with a conditional ballad, in which two strangers speculate on what it might be like *if* they were in love. So you get Billy and Julie doing 'If I Loved You' in *Carousel* and 'People Will Say We're In Love' in *Oklahoma!*. This isn't so very out of kilter with what happens in real life; it's only an externalized version of what you do in your head when you're on the Tube and there are no copies of the *Standard* lying about and the man sitting opposite you is under eighty, has all his limbs and isn't reading anything by L. Ron Hubbard.

The Moral Dimension

I once read a definition of kitsch as a 'denial of death'. Kitsch is a whitewash, a glazing over of the realities of life and insistence on a happy ending that amounts to a moral weakness. So Fagin, in the musical version of *Oliver!*, skips off into the sunset with Dodger when Dickens had him swinging from the gallows. Although the stage is littered with corpses at the end of *Les Misérables*, the first thing the survivors do is assemble a chorus to sing about how things will be better tomorrow.

The happy ending in a musical is often ambiguous, however. In *Gypsy*, at the end of the ostensibly upbeat anthem 'Everything's Coming Up Roses', there's a grinding, relentless edge to Ethel Merman's voice which betrays how much of the performance is a piece of empty cheerleading, done for her own benefit. The musical understands perfectly the gap between what people want from life and what they ultimately get; that is why even the happy songs are shot through with a kind of frustrated longing. And it's not true that all musicals end happily, as anyone who has attended the misguided effort to turn *Fiddler on the Roof* into a singalong production will know. (Singalong-a-pogrom, as we call it.)

Also: the shoddy sets, the mad singing and the weird dialogue are so dorky that they have to be sincere, and sincerity is the enemy of kitsch.

How To Make Men Love Musicals

What Would Barbra Do?

I have whittled down to five those musicals that stand the best chance of converting a hostile male audience to the charms of the genre. These are shows that rely heavily on *facts* and *politics* and don't refer too liberally to the changing of the seasons.

An obvious place to start is with those films that contain all the challenges of the musical – excessive costume, florid courtship, timid men and fiery women – but without the actual music. *The Way We Were* is a good bet because it even has Cold War politics, although anything with Barbra Streisand in it may prove too testing in the early days. *It's A Wonderful Life* gets good results because of James Stewart's credibility as a serious actor and all the time the film spends analysing the woes of the male condition. I tried out a male friend on *Gone With the Wind*, once, which I thought a clever move until two and a half hours in when Scarlett is standing on a hill behind Tara, clutching a root vegetable and vowing never to go hungry again and – imagine? – he moved to get up, as if *this were the end*. 'Ahh,' he said, in a brisk, humouring tone, 'that was great,' whereupon I told him to sit down and wipe the smile off his face, we were only halfway through.

Cabaret is probably the least painful actual musical to start with; strong on both politics and history and, if not exactly anti-romantic, then at least conscious of the self-delusional uses to which romance is put. It has literary credentials too, for the man who thinks himself Too Smart For Musicals. It was made in 1972 by Bob Fosse and starred Liza Minnelli and Michael York. Christopher Isherwood, on whose Berlin stories the film is based, didn't like it at all. He wrote in his diaries that Minnelli was 'clumsy and utterly wrong for the part', although 'touching sometimes, in a boyish good sport way'. And he thought the script cowardly in its treatment of the lead character's homosexuality, which the film presented, he wrote, 'as an indecent but comic weakness'. But as far as I can tell the film makes no moral distinction between homosexual and heterosexual promiscuity, both of which are shown to be welcome alternatives to Nazi ideas about romance.

In *Cabaret*, the songs mostly appear in the context of a public performance, i.e. are sung by people on stage or in an impromptu political rally in a beer garden rather than into each other's faces. Michael York isn't required to sing at all. The love affairs are doomed, there are no tedious dream sequences and the Nazis are violent and sinister rather than cartoon-like and dastardly, as in say *The Sound of Music*. Unlike the heroines of the golden era musicals, Sally Bowles is a complicated woman whose faux naivety, maintained at some cost in the face of Nazi aggression, is both courageous and evasive, silly and admirable, sentimental and strong-willed. *Cabaret* turns the traditional morality of the musical on its head: the people who pine about the future are the Hitler Youth. They are given a song to sing, 'Tomorrow Belongs To Me', in which Kander and Ebb take all the romantic clichés about hope and self-promotion and grasping the future and turn them into a Nazi anthem. Ambition is for fascists, they say; chaos is preferable to order; romance has an ugly side; we are all, to some extent, self-deceiving; it is merely a question of which deceptions we choose to sign up to.

Cabaret, which won eight Oscars in 1973, is so credible that purists think of it as a kind of traitor to the cause. It's just not uncool enough to be a real musical.

Guys and Dolls

If he gets on OK with *Cabaret* then it is time to move up a gear into an earlier age, the golden age, and there's an easy way in. There are no facts or politics in *Guys and Dolls* (1955), but there is Marlon Brando, singing with a devil-may-care attitude and wearing a sly grin that says call me a sissy and I'll break all your fingers. Frank Loesser's lyrics aren't the usual lovey-dovey fare, but are written in 1930s vernacular, a street musical precursor to *8 Mile* with a butch central theme: gambling.

The show is based on Damon Runyon's short stories of hoodlum New York, which are smart and snappy and hard to put down. They are, naturally, darker than the film version; in the original story 'The Idyll of Miss Sarah Brown', Sky Masterson is on the brink of murdering a man when he is saved by the loving intervention of the missionary doll. But something of the darkness remains in the film version – not in the gambling scenes, which are too jolly and stylized to be menacing, but in a quiet moment at the salsa club in Cuba, when Sky asks Sarah Brown what she wants from life and she delivers a pious little speech about the importance of being true to oneself. This is the staple conceit of the Rooney/Garland musicals and all the back-stage productions that came after them: that lurking behind one's dull exterior is a star, waiting to be born. Sky looks at Sarah Brown. And then he tells her that what she wants is not only impossible, but undesirable. It is a weird and powerful love scene, tearing aside for a second the idea that one should Be True To Oneself and Reach For The Sky and Never Give Up and savagely replacing it with another idea. Sky suggests that this notion that underneath one's cramped and dismal outer self a 'true' spirit languishes – a spirit which, were it not for the oppressive meddling of others, would be free to fly, soar, twinkle, come out of the dark and realize its potential through all the other clichés of bad songwriting – is totally bogus, a fantasy that allows people to stall indefinitely on actually doing anything while they sit around and mope, pretending they are wonderful; he implies that the stylized version of oneself, so self-consciously promoted elsewhere in *Guys and Dolls*, is one with the 'reality'. It is a downbeat note for a love scene – that things are what they are, not what we would like them to be – and yet it manages to be more romantic than all the usual effusions. At the end of the film, he tells Adelaide to stop holding out for Nathan to turn into somebody else and get smart to the idea that a person who acts unreliable and cowardly is an unreliable coward, not a reliable hero who tripped over and accidentally threw out all the wrong characteristics. So she loves an unreliable coward. So what?

The exchange in the bar in Cuba is the moment when the musical turns round and gives the dream it helped create a long, cold look. 'Being what you want,' says Sky to Sarah Brown. 'Nobody can, nobody does. If you could you probably wouldn't want to.' And they go outside to sing 'If I Were A Bell (I Would Ring)', which sounds, after the cold shower, like the sweetest song in the world.

What Would Barbra Do?

An American in Paris

There is something about Gene Kelly that has always given me the creeps. Perhaps it's the way he wears his trousers too high, or the fact that he was too old to carry off the kids' baseball cap he wore in *An American in Paris*. He does 'crazy' in a slightly Norman Wisdom, thumbs-up for the camera way. His dancing however is a good advertisement for masculinity and the musical, even though it is often used to illustrate girly love-sickness – in *An American in Paris* he dances around his Parisian garret actually singing that his heart goes 'pitter-pat'. But he does his best to make the moves look athletic, against what he saw as the feminization of his craft. Kelly once complained in an interview that 'dancing is a man's business, altogether, but women have taken it over' – and he built up his biceps to prove it.

West Side Story

With its knife-fights and street kids and self-conscious modernity, its classy score and great lyrics, *West Side Story* is supposed to be the big cross-over musical. It is supposed to appeal both to people who feel they are too highbrow for musicals and to those who think they are too cool for them. It's a beautiful show with beautiful music, but I've never been convinced by its hipness. Somehow the phoney swearing ('buggin'' for fucking) and ballet-style fight scenes make it seem squarer than its squarest rivals. Is it wrong to be pleased that, the year it came out, *The Music Man* beat it at the box office? A terrible recording of it was made by Kiri Te Kanawa and Jose Carreras in 1984 in which they undermined the whole idea of popular opera, by singing their parts in stiff, classical music style.

Paint Your Wagon

Two words: Clint Eastwood. If it's good enough for Eastwood to appear in a musical, it's good enough for whoever is giving you a hard time about it to watch one.

Brigadoon

I have a single, persuasive example of how this most unlovable of musicals forced a man I know to engage with the genre, through the power of sheer absurdity and a bit of phoney science. I finally saw *Brigadoon* for the first time last year and didn't shirk from asking the tough questions. Had it unfairly cheated *Seven Brides* of its budget for the location shoot? Had it squandered that money on silliness of such intensity that even my mother had been disgusted? What *was* Brigadoon? A man? A battle? A pub?

It turns out it's a place, sort of; a Scottish village which Gene Kelly and Van Johnson stumble across during a shooting trip to the Highlands. The year is 1954. They have come from New York and in the opening scene are shown reclining in the heather (but not in a gay way) discussing their love lives while keeping an eye out for grouse. Kelly plays Tommy Albright, a man who's not sure he's capable of loving any more. He's not sure what love is! Johnson plays Jeff Douglas, a professional cynic, who is always snorting and telling his friend to lighten up. They jog down the hill to the village where the people are wearing old-fashioned clothes and talking in accents that make Dick Van Dyke sound like Stanley Holloway.

'Good dee to yee,' says Cyd Charisse, walking past dragging a milk pail.

The villagers are singing a song called 'Down on MacConnachy Square', Angus MacGuffie and his assistant Meg, Harry, a young man who is in love with a village girl called Jean, and Cyd Charisse who plays Fiona. Jean is about to be married to a man called Charlie, in honour of which the village girls sing 'Waitin' For My Dearie', about the importance of marrying the right person.

Tommy and Jeff walk about in wonder. The only clue as to what is going on is an allusion dropped by a villager to a 'miracle', which when the New Yorkers enquire about it is batted away.

Tommy and Fiona walk through the heather up a hill, singing 'Heather on the Hill', an experience which makes Tommy wonder if there isn't more to life than the sophisticated but empty whirl of Manhattan. Back in the village, Jeff ('Oh, Mr Dooglass!') is being pursued by Meg, who invites him to her woodshed, but he's so knackered from all the excitement that he falls asleep and she sits, sinisterly rocking and knitting and smiling a secret smile while watching him slumber. At this point, *Brigadoon* starts to look like *The Wicker Man* with songs and Meg as favourite to light the bonfire.

Then Jean the bride packs up to move to her husband's house singing 'Jeannie's Packin' Up' and then Harry, who is still in love with her, calls round with a waistcoat for her father and has a bitter outburst at the door because not only is he losing the woman he loves, but owing to the 'miracle' he can't leave Brigadoon, which means he can't go to university but is condemned to a life of walking up and down the same street, trying to look busy. Harry shoves off, snarling, and Tommy and Fiona come down from the hill in love, then Tommy glimpses the family bible and sees that Fiona's birth date is 10 October 1722, which makes her 232 years old. Then he spies the entry for the wedding day, ink still wet on the page, and it reads 24 May 1746. Hang on a minute? Tommy is alarmed! Is this some kind of joke? Fiona sighs and says, go and ask Mr Lundie. Mr Lundie is the village elder whom they find sitting under a tree. He explains to Tommy about the miracle.

The village, it turns out, is charmed, because in the seventeenth century a Mr Forsythe climbed a hill and spoke to God and arranged that He would protect the village from the encroachment of modern values by ensuring that Brigadoon disappeared from the map – poof! – and that for every twenty-four-hour period that passed in the village, some one hundred years would pass in the world outside. In return for this, God required a sacrifice and old Mr Forsythe walked out into the heather to provide it. Mr Lundie says that since Mr Forsythe's pact with God, the village can now only appear in the real world once every hundred years and that if anyone leaves the village the spell will be broken and it will disappear for ever.

Tommy's mind is working overtime. So, he says, what if someone from the outside world wanted to live in the village . . . ? Mr Lundie says yes, that's possible, but it would mean never seeing anyone he knows in the modern world again.

What Would Barbra Do?

'If you love someone deeply enoof, anything is possible,' says Mr Lundie, to which Cyd Charisse replies gamely, 'Aye, anything is pussible. Good dee to yee.'

Then the wedding takes place, there's a tortuous sub-plot in which Harry gets shot trying to bolt from the village, and Tommy and Jeff just manage to escape over the bridge before nightfall and that is the end of that.

OK.

My thoughts about *Brigadoon* at this point are: that it's bad, but not as bad as I had expected. The score by Alan Jay Lerner and Frederick Loewe is a bit syrupy, Gene Kelly's voice is feeble and the accents are distractingly awful. But it's charming in a daft kind of way and there is at least one memorable song, 'Almost Like Being in Love'.

The second half gets under way. Tommy and Jeff are back in New York. Tommy is unhappy. He sits in a smart Manhattan cocktail joint, listening to his fiancée jaw on about arrangements for their wedding, while replaying in his mind the image of Cyd Charisse singing 'Waitin' For My Dearie' and 'Dinna Ye Know'. His fiancée is rich and bossy and the film throws its full weight against her. Tommy asks himself, what really matters in life? The pull on his heart strings is all the answer he needs. He gets up abruptly from the table, breaks off his engagement, rings Jeff and tells him he's going back to Scotland. Jeff says, are you crazy? Do you really want to live in an eighteenth-century village for the rest of your life? But there is no talking Tommy out of it.

He flies back to Scotland with Jeff in loyal pursuit and starts tramping the Highlands in search of the village. He walks and walks, searching in vain, until in an echo of King Lear's breakdown on the heath he looks up at the heavens and cries, 'God! Why do people have to lose things to find out what they really mean?'

And then, through the mist, a little stone kissing bridge appears. On the other side is old Mr Lundie, with a twinkly look on his face. He reminds Tommy that anything is possible if you're in love, even miracles, and while Jeff stands open-mouthed Tommy pops over the bridge and disappears, presumably for ever.

And that's it. Now. As the credits roll, my first thought is: if no one can get into the village and no one get out of it, there are issues of inbreeding that the film has chosen to ignore. Secondly: logistics. How is it that Brigadoon is still accessible from the modern-day world of 1954? Surely, if each day in Brigadoon is worth one hundred years in the real world, by the time Gene Kelly makes it back to Scotland the year in the outside world compared to that in the village should be at least a thousand years later. If the film's only answer to this is the line 'anything is possible' then my mother was quite right: it is the stupidest, most unbelievably badly plotted musical of all time.

I am working up a rage about this when my friend Oliver (position on musicals: they'd be fine if it wasn't for the music) rings. I give him a brief plot outline and ask him what he thinks.

'Surely the first problem,' says Oliver, 'is that when they leave Brigadoon in the first place, it's still 1954.'

'No,' I say, 'because they leave before nightfall.'

'Hang on,' he says, 'you mean that during the day, time passes in Brigadoon at the same rate as it does outside?'

'Yes.'

'So the relationship between time outside and time in Brigadoon isn't a constant?'

'No. It all happens at midnight.'

Oliver laughs long and hard and not altogether kindly. Ten minutes later he sends an email.

Oliver's email

A further clue may be offered in the lyrics to the Waterboys' 'The Whole Of The Moon': the person being addressed (who 'saw the whole of the moon') also 'saw Brigadoon' – clearly someone with special powers of perception in general relative to the human average.

This might point towards an answer according to which the perceived difference in time was somehow a property of the observer.

Otherwise, the key question is – if time in the outside world advances by one hundred years every midnight in Brigadoon, why do the residents of the outside world not perceive a sudden jump in time every so often? Or does Brigadoon's position in time relative to the outside world move forward by one hundred years every midnight? That would seem to amount to the same effect for the residents of Brigadoon, without causing odd effects for everyone else – but it would not really achieve the goals of the original deal, since the influences of modernity would presumably threaten Brigadoon (to the extent that they can do so) one hundred times faster and more alarmingly.

My reply
See what fun a musical can be?!

Oliver's reply
It would make far more sense, I think, for the original deal to have been that time in Brigadoon will advance at 1/100th of the speed of time in the outside world, but that the residents will somehow perceive it to advance at the normal speed.

When I see him a week later he says, 'Of course, there's a further possibility: that Brigadoon is positioned somehow outside the known world.'

'What do you mean?'

Oliver gets a look on his face like Tom Cruise during his you-can't-handle-the-truth speech in *A Few Good Men*.

'I mean, it's possible that time passes differently just by virtue of Brigadoon's being a long way from earth.'

'You mean in space?' I say.

'Well . . .' he says.

'Mate.' I'm annoyed now. 'It's not that kind of film.'

Alan Jay Lerner and Frederick Loewe also wrote the music for *My*

Fair Lady, *Gigi* and *Paint Your Wagon*, but they lost their touch with *Brigadoon*. Gene de Paul meanwhile, a much less well known songwriter, fluked a brilliant score for *Seven Brides for Seven Brothers*. Where *Seven Brides* is good-hearted and unpretentious, *Brigadoon* is tediously moralizing. To my mother's great satisfaction, *Seven Brides* was the runaway hit of 1954 and *Brigadoon*, with its fancy breaches in the space/time continuum, limped home a poor second.

'If they want to disregard two hundred years of human bing-bang, so be it,' says Jeff Douglas, against whose cynicism Tommy is supposed to shine as an example of a man who knows what's important in this life, and it isn't good coffee. But it turns out – and this is my point about fans of the musical, they're not as sappy as you think – that everyone in the audience agreed with the other guy.

Women Who Love Musicals

What Would Barbra Do?

I suppose the name Gaylord Ravenal wasn't funny at the time, which was 1927, when *Show Boat* was adapted from a book by the novelist Edna Ferber about an old Mississippi river boat and the people who lived on her. 'From the book by Edna Ferber,' my mother would say, with great authority, whenever *Show Boat* came on. It was one of her favourites on account of all that noble suffering it espoused and also the position it took on racism, advanced for the time of its writing (1926), still advanced at the time of its second filming (1951) and with lingering advancedness when I first saw it in the 1980s, when a mixed race relationship mightn't lose you your job in the town where we lived, but would certainly get you stares in the library.

I start snivelling in the first frame of *Show Boat*. It has something to do with Howard Keel, his solid, genial manner and slightly protuberant teeth. Call him the poor man's Mario Lanza if you will, but I have a lot of time for Keel. I like the way he sings his numbers as if to the hard of hearing and is always right up against the buttons of his shirt.

When I think of Keel it's not as Gaylord Ravenal in *Show Boat*, or Adam Pontipee in *Seven Brides for Seven Brothers* or even as Clayton in *Dallas*. It's as Petruchio in *Kiss Me Kate*, standing centre stage in a full-length brown leotard, hands on hips and singing a song in which the ancient Italian city of Padua is contrived to rhyme with the line 'mad, you are'. Even without Ann Miller standing beside him with a flowerpot on her head this would have been a tough scene; but Keel pulled it off. He was all class.

When Jerome Kern and Oscar Hammerstein, just thirty-one at the time, wrote *Show Boat* it was the first musical to integrate songs and plot and to present a view of life that wasn't all high kicks and champagne. They and Richard Rodgers had been muttering for a while that it was time the musical comedy faced up to the facts of life and from Ferber, a women's rights activist and one of the few female members of the Algonquin Round Table, they took a story about life in the seedy underbelly of the American dream. (Ferber would go on to write the novel on which the film *Giant*, starring James Dean, was based.)

The principal storyline in *Show Boat* is a conventional enough romance in which Magnolia, the daughter of parents who own a theatrical riverboat called the *Cotton Blossom*, elopes with Gaylord Ravenal, a good-for-nothing gambler. But the sub-plot revolves around the issue of miscegenation – not, I should imagine, a very sexy word to theatregoers of the late 1920s, who turned up expecting the usual frolics and instead got the story of a boozy showgirl called Julie who gets kicked out of work on the discovery she is mixed-race and married to a white man.

The debut performance was on 27 December 1927 at the Ziegfeld Theater and was greeted, after the curtain fell, with stunned silence. Producer Florenz Ziegfeld had his head in his hands; the show was a tremendous gamble. But the next day, the reviews were ecstatic.

I have seen *Show Boat* on stage a couple of times, but nothing matches the film version. In the opening scene, Keel strolls by the banks of the Mississippi singing 'I Drift Along with My Fancy', although it's clear that he doesn't – Keel was badly miscast as Gaylord Ravenal; it is Omar Sharif in *Funny Girl* who looks like the real thing, a no-good gambling rat with five o'clock shadow and an air of disgust and self-pity. And yet there's something about Keel's attempt to play tragedy that makes the whole thing even more heartbreaking. The real star of the show is Ava 'perhaps it's the whisky talking' Gardner, the best end of the night role model a girl can have, in a red sequin dress and that look on her face like there's no way back now you may as well pour me another, as she stands on the dock and blows a kiss at the departing *Cotton Blossom* and has nothing to look forward to but a life of booze and unkind men and memories and that pincushion Kathryn Grayson gave her when she left the boat, it was meant to be for Christmas but . . . It reminds me of a line from Toni Morrison's *The Bluest Eye*, about the world in all its 'waste and beauty'.

The great thing about *Show Boat* is that it loses no time getting stuck into tragedy. It isn't long after Keel and Magnolia's elopement that he loses all their money gambling and gives her his You're Better Off Without Me speech. Magnolia tells him he's a weak man, 'weak, weak, weak', and then it cuts to Julie singing drunkenly at the piano about her good-for-nuthin' Bill – she used to dream she'd wind up with a man with a 'giant brain' and a 'noble head', which is a rather frightening image, but got stuck with this loser instead; in any case, she loves him – and later, in her dressing room, she hears Noley auditioning badly out front and runs away so that the club owners have no choice but to hire her as a last-minute replacement. And then on New Year's Eve, Noley comes out on stage and starts singing in a whisper and gets heckled by the crowd until her dad tells everyone to shut up and she catches sight of him in the front row and with tears in his eyes he says 'Remember what I told ya, *smile*' and she smiles even though she's crying and lifts her voice and Wins Them Round and brings the house down and returns with her dad to the *Cotton Blossom*. And meanwhile Gaylord Ravenal is on a riverboat somewhere and hears a woman at the piano singing drunkenly 'Can't Help Loving That Man' (which incidentally Vera Lynn once cut a recording of, opting for the folk pronunciation of 'dat man', to strange and unhappy effect) and the man she's with slaps her and Ravenal punches him and she thanks him and he says, someone I once loved sang that song and storms off. And Julie thinks Hang On A Minute and asks the barman the name of the man and he tells her: Gaylord Ravenal. So she chases him onto the deck and berates him for abandoning his pregnant wife in her hour of need and he is stunned – 'on my oath' he says, he never knew she was pregnant – and Julie fishes out a newspaper clipping from her pocket with a picture of Noley and her daughter Kim on it and Ravenal resolves to go back and do the right thing and as he's leaving Julie grabs him and, swaying tragically, from the booze or the boat or a combination of the two, says, 'Don't tell her you saw me . . . like this.' And it's like that bit in *Gone With the Wind* when Melanie is in the coach with Belle Watling, who gives her some money for the war effort and Melanie thanks her and says that in spite of being a woman of the night she has a good and noble heart and Belle gets tears in her eyes and says, 'Miz Wilkes, you is a real lady,' i.e. not trash like that Scarlett O'Hara.

Then Ravenal comes back and he's made a load of money and sings 'Only Make Believe' to the little girl He Never Knew He Had, fairly bellows in her face, it's a wonder she doesn't scream, and then his voice cracks, not very convincingly, it's not Keel's way, but still he has a go and the family reunites and Kathryn Grayson trills out a song in her ear-bending soprano. And Julie's alone, quite alone, looking out at the Mississippi with that same mixture of self-pity and defiance you get in all great tragic heroines, with only the knowledge she saved Noley between her and outright desolation. And Noley Never Knew of Julie's Great Sacrifice, even though Julie was pretty much washed up by then anyway, but there was still tenderness in her heart for the memory of the life she once led and Noley Never Knew but oh, At Least She's Happy Now and Julie's Sacrifice Was Not In Vain. And the final frame of the film is *not* the happy, reunited couple on the deck of the *Cotton Blossom*, but Julie standing alone at the quay, seeing her happiness evaporate to the strains of 'Ol' Man River'.

Show Boat is a retort to the accusation that all musicals are light and fluffy and contractually obliged to end happily. Although the casting of Gardner, who looked about as mixed race as Yul Brynner looked Siamese, was spineless, the role of the slave, Joe, was one of the first in which a black man was permitted to express anything other than happiness at the way in which his country was treating him. Paul Robeson's 1936 performance of 'Ol' Man River' became talismanic in light of what happened to Robeson in the years afterwards, when his support for the Soviet Union abroad and his civil rights activism at home would result in years of persecution by the US government.

Gardner meanwhile became one with the role she played, increasingly bitter and deranged and prone, in long, alcoholic interviews, to raging against the studios for wrecking her career. 'I have been a movie star for twenty-five years,' she told Rex Reed in 1968, 'and I've got nothing, *nothing* to show for it. All I've got is three lousy ex-husbands.' She bad-mouthed her roles as Eloise in *Mogambo*, Jean in *The Hucksters* and Sarah in the epic 1966 flick *The Bible*, of which she would only say, 'How could anybody stay married for a hundred years to *Abraham*, who was one of the biggest bastards who ever lived?'

It isn't big or clever to drink yourself to death and nostalgia for that period of filmmaking overlooks how miserable so many of the people involved in it seem to have been. Still, you can't help feeling that compared to today's gym-obsessed stars, there was something heroic about Gardner and the manner of her downfall, as there had been about the manner of her ascent: from a childhood in backwoods North Carolina, where her family were share-croppers on a tobacco farm, to one of the biggest stars in Hollywood. In her memoir, her friend Esther Williams recalled sadly that when tipsy at parties Gardner would say to her, 'You don't want to talk to me, I'm just trailer trash.' Of all the films she made, *Show Boat* was the one she said she really cared about. In an effort to sing authentically she had gone to the same voice coach as Dorothy Dandridge and Lena Horne, who had lost out to her in auditions. But in the final cut, MGM dubbed over her with a pearly white soprano. 'Hell, what a mess,' she said in 1968. 'They wasted God knows how many thousands of dollars and ended up with crap.'

After her stroke in 1989 her ex-husband Frank Sinatra paid all her medical bills and when she died in 1990, her dog went to Gregory Peck. How could it have been otherwise?

Somewhere between *Show Boat* and *Lethal Weapon III* romance went out of fashion. All that la-la-la was blamed for raising little girls' expectations so high that when they found out love wasn't really a Mickey Rooney barn dance, they were so disappointed not even shoulder pads and a career in the City could save them. In this light, the heroes of golden age musicals looked like boorish pigs and the women like doormats. Lines such as 'Personally I think a little physical punishment is good for people once in a while' (John Raitt, in *The Pajama Game*) or Jane Powell in *Seven Brides for Seven Brothers* dreaming of a time when she might cook for one, 'just one!' man, or that bit at the end of *Carousel* in which Shirley Jones, in her role as battered wife Julie, wonders if it's possible for someone to 'hit you, real loud and hard' and for it to actually feel as if he'd kissed you (no Shirley, that's why it's called acting) – none of this went down well in the war against biological determinism and the arbitrary gender construct.

In musicals of the golden age the men are called things like Cable or Brackett or Lockwood or Truett, names which imply not only structural integrity but strength and an ability to pin things down.

Women Who Love Musicals

The women are called diminutives like Kathy or Laurey or Nellie, with cute alliterative surnames that don't have a hard syllable between them. I know Mitzi Gaynor couldn't help the fact that in real life her name made her sound like the winner of the toy group at Crufts, but it didn't help reverse the impression that while the men in musicals were holding things together, the women just stood by and yapped. Women over a certain age in these productions don't even have surnames; they are identified purely by their relationship to other, more important characters and made to sit behind butter churns (Aunt Eller in *Oklahoma!*) or do voodoo (Bloody Mary in *South Pacific*) or live exclusively through their children (Rose in *Gypsy*). At least Cousin Netty in *Carousel* is allowed to run a successful small business. But she isn't allowed to enjoy it. When her niece, Julie, is having marital problems, Cousin Netty summons the wisdom of her long, sad life serving seafood to folk in couples and says, 'The main thing is to keep on living.' Judging by the look on her face, if living is its own reward then it's a small one. Aunt Eller delivers a similarly grim speech in *Oklahoma!* when she tells the heroine that life is something to be overcome and you can only overcome it by being hearty. This means making light of the fact that, in the musicals of the 1950s, there is no worse fate than to be a woman over a certain age, alone in the world. That is why the goal of all women below a certain age, in musicals, is to marry.

Most women I know of my age aren't exactly what you'd call romantic. These are women in their late twenties and early thirties who can't tolerate a commitment that lasts longer than the *EastEnders* omnibus; who say 'Get off' when a man tries to hold their hand in public; who, when he offers to drive them to the airport, look at him as if he has confessed to participating in genocide.

'He offered to take me to the airport.'

'Ugh! Gross!'

It is the women rather than the men I know who don't reply to amorous text messages for days; who will kick someone out at 4 a.m. on the coldest night of the year because they can't be bothered to have a conversation with him the following morning. Faced, once, with the problem of someone whose company was nice while it lasted, but was lasting too long into the next morning, I did the only thing I knew was guaranteed to shift him. Getting out of bed I fetched my iBook, paged through iTunes, went back into the bedroom and, holding the thing clam-like over his head, activated at top volume the theme to *Oklahoma!*. It came out in such a long, piercing howl – 'O-o-o-o-o-o-o-klahoma' – that even I was a bit shocked. He opened one eye, so wide and terrified that it looked like a cartoon eyeball straining at a keyhole. 'Who *are* you?' he whispered.

And yet a lot of women my age love musicals. They even love *Gigi*, the 1958 adaptation of the novel by Colette in which seventeen-year-old Leslie Caron is presented as a courtesan to Louis Jourdan by her own family, while Maurice Chevalier makes eyes at small girls in the background; even *Funny Face*, in which Audrey Hepburn abandons her ambitions to better herself to take up with doddery old Fred Astaire – way too ancient in 1957 to be playing opposite the young

Hepburn. It is hard to figure out why this is. I remember a friend saying to me once, 'Is it just that they are old and we hold them to lower standards?' We looked at each other in alarm. What if all that stuff, chicks and ducks and eyes and blossom, which, without thinking about too much, we had always assumed was anchored to something a bit steelier and more worthwhile – because otherwise why would we keep going back to it – was in reality all there was? What if it was in the same category as Celine Dion? That couldn't be right, could it?

My friend Mark was at a dinner with his wife recently when the subject of what they allowed their children to watch on TV came up. They tutted with everyone else about the influence of violent cartoons and junk food advertising and then their hosts said that, of course, they wouldn't let their children watch *The Sound of Music*, because it was sexist. 'No,' said Mark gravely, 'absolutely not,' and his wife nodded in solemn agreement and in the car afterwards they looked at each other and screamed, *What?* 'She defeated the Nazis for God's sake,' said Mark. 'She wasn't in the kitchen baking.'

It's easy to figure out the appeal to modern women of the early musicals. In the black and white productions of the '20s and '30s Ginger Rogers is always telling Fred Astaire to sling his hook until the last frame. While he mills about looking bored, or dances in a beautiful, louche fashion, she hurls herself about until the sweat pours, her tap shoes sounding on the floor like carpentry. The sort of women Rogers played in the 1930s would, on being told how nice they looked, reply with an ungracious 'I know'. They would dispense nuggets of hard-bitten wisdom from one side of their mouths and nod to the arbitrary nature of femininity, as Hélène Cixous might put it, with lines such as 'Connie, women weren't born with silk stockings, you know.' Only at the end of each film would a piece of conventional 1930s knot-tying be forced on the plot and with it the inevitable end of the heroine's career. The studio recycled storylines so shamelessly that it is hard to remember one plot line from another. More than the compromise of the ending, what you remember is Rogers's haughty face telling Fred Astaire to bugger off, she has better things to do.

Musicals of the golden age are a bit trickier. *Seven Brides for Seven Brothers* looks vile on paper, so much so that you wonder whether, during filming, anyone on the crew raised a hand and asked if the premise for the film wasn't in slightly, er, bad taste. It retells the legend of the rape of the Sabine women, in which the women of a mountain community outside Rome are kidnapped and forced into marriage by Roman soldiers in a drive to quickly populate the empire. It was set down by Livy in the first century BC, retold by Plutarch in the second century AD and has been depicted through the ages by Rubens, Poussin, Picasso and, in 1954, Howard Keel, who summarized the story in a jolly number called 'Sobbin' Women'. In a sort of anthem to no-means-yes, he sang of how, although the women acted 'angry' and 'annoyed,' when it came down to it they were secretly 'overjoyed'.

Johnny Mercer made an easy listening version of 'Sobbin' Women', which is one of the creepiest records ever made. But for some reason Howard Keel gets away with it. It's partly because *Seven Brides* is so preposterous that it seems churlish to be offended by it. And while

Jane Powell drags herself around like a drudge for a while at the beginning, before long she is running the show. It's not until you've heard the director, Stanley Donen, singing 'I'm the Queen of the May' in an outtake that you realize how little the men in *Seven Brides* have in common with the Roman legion. A man can't really be accused of upholding the patriarchy when he stands in stick-on red sideburns and two inches of makeup, singing about spring.

I don't mean to mount a feminist re-reading of golden age musicals, although I'm sure it can be (and probably has been) done. But I do like to think that, like the Tevye in *Fiddler on the Roof*, when it comes to sexual politics they are liberals straining to burst out of conservative clothing.

Carousel

It used to worry me that one of my favourite musicals was *Carousel*, starring lovable wife-beater Billy Bigelow. That bit at the end gets me every time: when he comes down from heaven to attend his daughter's graduation and stands next to his wife Julie who is lit by his ghostly presence and he's had what amounts to a crisis of masculinity up there, but has pulled through to whisper in Julie's ear with all the feeling in the world, 'Know that I loved you, Julie; know that I loved you!' – this guy, who could never say the words when he was alive for fear of seeming weak, and Julie smiles, ignited, and the daughter sits and listens with tears in her eyes as the headmaster, who looks a lot like the star-maker, tells the class that the only way to happiness is neither to dwell on their parents' failures ('Listen, darlin'!' whispers

Billy urgently in her ear), nor to lean on their successes, but to understand that the world belongs to them as much as to the next fella and the bells of the carousel twinkle ruthlessly on in a key that doesn't suggest things will turn out all right, but you've just got to hope, haven't you. It breaks my heart. But surely I should be booing.

In most Rodgers and Hammerstein films, the goodies are unspeakably good and the baddies unspeakably bad. Jud Fry, the bad guy in *Oklahoma!*, lives in the smokehouse at the bottom of Aunt Eller's garden, where he hatches evil plans to win the heroine and slavers over porn. (Even though he burned down the house of his last employer and killed everyone in it, I always felt sorry for Jud. Typical that he should be the only swarthy-looking guy in the whole thing; and the distinction made between his sexual interest in women and the neutered desire of the leading men showed the musical at its anodyne worst.)

In *The Sound of Music* it's a no-brainer of nuns versus Nazis and in *South Pacific* the bad guy is the entire Japanese army, which lingers in the wings to remind us that, while American society might be a bit racist now and then, it's not as bad as those imperial yellow rat bastards.

Morally speaking, *Carousel* is a lot more complicated than all of these. It is adapted from the play *Liliom* by Hungarian dramatist Ferenc Molnar, a Jew who fled Nazi persecution in Hungary during the war. Molnar was influenced by Pirandello and Oscar Wilde and in *Liliom* told the bleak tale of a violent man who assaults his wife, dies and winds up in purgatory, where he is given a shot at redemption. Fritz Lang made a

French-language version of it in 1934, much darker, unsurprisingly, than the Hollywood one, in which Liliom, or Billy Bigelow as he became, is condemned to eternal damnation if he fails in his mission to put things right back on earth. (In an even earlier, grimmer version made in 1930, he spent those years actually being toasted in Hell.)

There was no eternal hellfire in the Hollywood version, just a twinkly heaven with dry ice and stars on strings and an avuncular old guy, the 'star-maker', who runs the show. In the original play, his role was performed by stern celestial policemen.

Still, for a musical, it is pretty rough stuff. Nora Ephron's screenwriting parents, Henry and Phoebe, didn't let Billy off the hook in their script; most of the responsibility for what happens is placed on his shoulders. The action is moved from Budapest to turn of the century New England, where the hero is a barker on a carousel and summarized by the local policeman as 'a pretty fly gazebo'. After marrying the heroine, he loafs about, sponging off Cousin Netty and half-heartedly considering a life of crime. In the seven-minute soliloquy Billy sings on the beach, he wrestles with his good and bad angels, trying to imagine what his unborn child will be like, and vowing to pull himself together and stop being such a bad-tempered layabout. Gene Kelly was considered for the part originally, but was replaced by Gordon MacRae when the demands of the role became apparent. At the end of the soliloquy, Bigelow realizes that apart from working on a carousel he has no marketable skills and so, with agonizing reluctance, decides to say yes to his mate Jigger's suggestion that they stage a robbery.

What Would Barbra Do?

In the play, Liliom commits suicide after the robbery fails. Billy Bigelow isn't allowed to do that in the film. Instead he falls on his knife and as he slips away, with Julie by his side, he is still talking cobblers about the plans he has to make good and move to San Francisco . . . 'Hold my hand tight. Tighter! Tighter still!' Poor, self-aggrandizing Billy Bigelow.

The point is that here is a musical, bang in the middle of the golden age, in which the hero is a self-loathing wife-beater and the moral of the story is that life is a bit scummy and full of unresolved longing, for which it places much of the blame on the male ego. When Billy gets into trouble, it is partly because society is shown to have no tolerance for outsiders, partly because of the pressure it puts on people to be successful and partly because of his own, stupid male pride: he won't get a job on a herring boat and earn a decent living. The boat is owned by a character called Enoch Snow, who represents Polite Society and who one is encouraged to take against. When he and his wife Carrie are courting, she has to pull off the lyric 'fish is my favourite perfume' in defence of her fiancé's body odour, and his effeminate laugh and ridiculous moustache – not a manly one like Howard Keel's, but a Dali-esque handlebar job – are designed to make him seem stupid.

You know you are supposed to hate Enoch Snow when he scoffs at his wife for preferring a Broadway show to *Julius Caesar*.

Secondary couples in the golden age musical must be either very silly, like the Snows, or very tragic, like Tuptim and Lun in *The King and I*, or Lieutenant Cable and Liat in *South Pacific*. It is their job to make the principal couple look better by being extremists of some kind, either ultra-rebels or ultra-conformists, and they are often required to fail in their romantic endeavours because, dramatically speaking, if everyone's ambitions are allowed to succeed, then success doesn't mean anything.

The Snows create a context for Billy Bigelow's anger at the world without excusing it. It's not ideal that, instead of taking out a restraining order against him, Julie Jordan puts on a martyred expression and gets going on lunch. But if you overlook the kiss me/hit me line at the end of the film, she isn't uncritical of her husband's behaviour. In the song 'What's the Use of Wond'rin'?' she describes the momentum that takes hold in a relationship and makes it impossible to leave, even when common sense tells you it's the only thing to do.

Annie Get Your Gun

Worse than *Seven Brides for Seven Brothers*, worse than *Gigi*, worse than *Carousel* by a long shot is *Annie Get Your Gun*, the dodgiest of the dodgy '50s musicals. It was produced by Arthur Freed, with a score by Irving Berlin and lyrics by Herbert and Dorothy Fields, and was based on the real life story of Annie Oakley, raised Phoebe Ann Mozee, in Darke County, Ohio. She was the fifth of eleven children and at the age of nine, after her father died, started hunting to help feed her family. She became known as a talented marksman and at a contest in Cincinnati, Ohio, beat Frank E. Butler, whom she wound up marrying. Together they toured with Buffalo Bill's Wild West Show in which Oakley was advertised as Little Miss Sure Shot. It was said that her aim was so fine that she once shot the ashes off the cigar of Kaiser Wilhelm II of Germany. In 1901 she was badly injured in a train crash, but recovered, then had a car crash, but recovered, and died at the age of sixty-six, of anaemia, in 1926.

Twenty years later, a musical was written of her life in which much was made of the damage done to Frank's ego by his sweetheart's superior gun skills. He became the sharp-shooter who could only fall for a woman once he'd proved her to be inferior to him. In order to get her man, Oakley had to fluff a shooting contest and pretend to be second best.

It opened on Broadway in 1946 with Ethel Merman as Annie and Ray Middleton as Frank Butler and was made into a film four years later starring Howard Keel and Betty Hutton, the last-minute replacement for Garland. I first saw *Annie Get Your Gun* in the West End in the 1980s and recall watching the stage in disbelief as Annie Oakley, played by '70s rocker Suzi Quatro, was exhorted by Chief Sitting Bull to be second best. During the crucial shooting contest, when she deliberately messes up so that Frank Butler can win and feel secure enough to marry her, my mother sat beside me loudly tutting. At the end she said, 'You see?' and looked crossly at my dad, who as far as I knew had never made anyone forfeit a shooting contest to conserve his male pride.

But, and here's the thing, far from endorsing Frank Butler's position, my mother thought *Annie Get Your Gun* did a fine job of exposing him and the reality of things generally, i.e. that women go about constantly indulging men's egos. The show wasn't a place marker for the patriarchy at all, she thought, but a loud critique of it and the contortions it forced women into.

'But why couldn't she win?' I asked.

'Because he was weak,' she said.

'But she should have—'

'I know,' she snapped, 'it's sad and unfair. But what matters is she was still better.'

Getting The Joke

Getting The Joke

It is one of the timeless, unvarying rules of the universe, that a man who can talk for twenty minutes in the pub about his enthusiasm for Barbra Streisand's 1973 classic 'The Way We Were', is not a man intent, later that evening, on making advances. You're on pretty safe ground, I'd say, in such a context, to express your enthusiasm for that man without it being misconstrued by another man, his friend, who might be standing next to him and with whom you might or might not be on a sort of date.

'It's that fight they have about Communism,' sighs the first man, who is all in black and has nicely trimmed fingernails, 'when Robert Redford says to Babs, "they're just principles," and Babs says, "Hubble, people *are* their principles." God, I love it.'

'I love *you*,' you might say, guilelessly, and plant a little kiss on his cheek. 'We have to be friends for ever.'

Later that evening, as you stand alone on the pavement, abandoned by your date, you might wonder what exactly went wrong.

I guess I was just unlucky. Because, even though straight men are getting gayer by the day, there is still generally a cut-off at the passion-for-musicals stage that preserves it as a test of his leanings. Not all gay men love musicals, of course. There are a few who seem to hate them because liking them is such a cliché.

'It's such a cliché to like musicals,' my friend Ritchie's boyfriend always groans to him.

'Hon,' says Ritchie, 'you've got a shaved head, tattoos and an earring. The time for worrying about clichés has passed.'

I maintain that Ritchie's affection for musicals is no deeper than mine. But, as with all male nerds, Ritchie has a memory for incidental detail that I just can't compete with. 'Do you remember that stage production of *Guys and Dolls* with Bob Hoskins and the guy from *Chariots of Fire* who died?' he'll throw in casually over lunch. Or, 'D'you remember the original *Starlight Express* had that guy from *Shalamar* in it, who did the body-popping?' Or, 'Apparently Charmian Carr asked Julie Andrews what she should do with the money she'd earned from *The Sound of Music*. And Julie said, *buy a fur coat*.'

'Anyway,' you'll say, trying to recover some ground, 'the best Adelaide was Julia McKenzie in the National Theatre production of *Guys and Dolls* in 1982.' (That's not how I said it, exactly, because I've had to look up the date.)

'Oh, she was marvellous. But the Imelda Staunton version in '96 was good, too.' (That's how he said it, exactly, date-inclusive.)

Ritchie has very pronounced views about the rights and wrongs of musical staging. The Ewan McGregor production of *Guys and Dolls* in the West End, for example, which was almost universally well reviewed, was to Ritchie's mind, 'terrible' because of its trendy, minimalist staging. 'I don't want a classy reinterpretation,' he said with disgust. The production of *Thoroughly Modern Millie* starring Amanda Holden – 'well, I'm sorry darling, but it suffered from the cheap-sets problem as well.' He has no time for Rex Harrison. 'I hate speak-singing. If you can't fucking sing, don't appear in a musical.'

The centre of the universe for Ritchie is a shop called Dress Circle, in Covent Garden. It has the world's most comprehensive collection of musicals soundtracks and memorabilia. Occasionally, when I have had a rough day, I go in there and just wander about, touching the Connie Francis CDs and drawing comfort from the presence of the moustachioed man behind the counter. I might ask him something, like when the US import of *Frank Sinatra: Live At The Sands* is expected in, and he will reply in a kindly and authoritative fashion.

Like most of us, Ritchie doesn't introspect about his taste unless specifically asked to. 'I don't know,' he says vaguely, 'I just like them.' When pressed, he supposes that it has something to do with the fact that when he was growing up in the 1970s, his mum used to do the hoovering to Barbra Streisand LPs. 'Funny,' says Ritchie, 'I never thought to blame her for my homosexuality.' He remembers being at home at Christmas as a miserable, closeted teenager and the *Wizard of Oz* coming on TV, offering such escape and relief and the promise of a world of possibility, that his taste in music never looked back. Fifteen years later he appeared as the Cowardly Lion in an amateur production of the *Wizard of Oz*. I won't go near amateur musicals, but Ritchie has a stronger stomach. 'Oh, I've seen some terrible shows,' he says. 'There was one in Essex with a fat boy playing Oliver Twist. "Please sir, I want some more." No, bugger off, you've had enough.'

Notice how many of the most charged scenes in a musical aren't between the principal man and woman, but between same-sex characters singing to each other of their love for absent partners. The most poignant moment of *The King and I* is the song that Lady Thiang sings to Deborah Kerr, petitioning her on the dying king's behalf. In *South Pacific*, Rossano Brazzi and John Kerr who plays Cable look into each other's eyes and duet, prettily, about their love for absent women. I'm not suggesting Josh Logan, the director, set out to be homoerotic, but that is the end result. It reminds me of the story Gore Vidal tells about the making of *Ben-Hur*, during which the director William Wyler chose to introduce a note of homoerotic tension between Charlton Heston, the male lead, and his friend Massala, played by Stephen Boyd. Boyd was told to flirt outrageously during their scenes together and the crew told to shoot it accordingly. But at all costs, said Wyler, 'nobody tell Charlton.'

The role played by camp in musicals is often misunderstood. There is a bit in Arthur Miller's novella *Plain Girl*, when the heroine describes a look she sometimes catches on people's faces when she turns to greet them at a party. It is not a flattering look; frank disappointment. She concludes that there must be a gap between the expectations raised by the back of her head and the reality of the face peering out the front of it and, as a result, she cultivates an air of amused detachment, a mild irony which, as she turns round to greet people says, yes, I know, funny isn't it?

When I read that passage it reminded me of something and I couldn't remember what. Then I got it: it's the attitude of the leading lady in all those films in which the pretty girl is defeated by the girl with the look of mild irony on her face which seems to say, yes, I know, funny isn't it? It's in *Singin' in the Rain*, in which jolly but plain (well, relatively speaking) Kathy Selden defeats beautiful but thick Lina Lamont; it's in *Easter Parade*, in which chipper but plain Hannah Brown defeats beautiful but boring Nadine Hale; it's in *Gypsy*, in which ungainly but interesting Gypsy Rose Lee defeats pretty but screechy Baby June; it's in *Cabaret*, in which Sally Bowles doesn't defeat anyone, but is pretty weird-looking for a leading lady. Even in *High Society*, in which Grace Kelly radiates top of the tree beauty as the heroine Tracy, it is Celeste Holm, wise-cracking in the supporting role, for whom the film reserves its sympathies.

I thought about all this and then I wondered if that isn't a big part of why so many women love musicals; not for the songs or the romance, but because once dubbing went out of fashion, musicals had no choice but to value talented heroines over merely beautiful ones. Then I thought, perhaps all good musicals are actually anti-musicals. (I wondered briefly if this meant anything.) And *then* I thought maybe that's why drag queens raid them for their acts, because of this air of detachment from the leading ladies who are not, in the circumstances, quite as beautiful as they ought to be. I don't know. It's just an idea.

By the standards of the rest of the world, of course, these women are hardly hunchbacks of Notre Dame. But by the standards of 1950s and early 1960s Hollywood, they were pretty third division. The mildly subversive tone they introduced into musical films of the era is not camp in the *Rocky Horror Show* sense, but it is still a form of camp. It's Judy Garland telling Chuck Walters, the director of *Easter Parade*, 'Look sweetie, I'm no June Allyson, you know. Don't get cute with me. None of that batting-the-eyelids bit or the fluffing the hair routine for me, buddy!' It's Lana Turner in the 1941 backstage musical *Ziegfeld Girl* saying, 'Listen, honey, being a

Ziegfeld Girl is swell, but it's only going to last a couple of years and then what? I'd give anything for a man with a station wagon. And you've got a guy with a truck!' (At the end of the movie, Turner suffers a breakdown and retires from the theatre to raise ducks.)

You see it in *Meet Me in St Louis*, a potentially saccharine film about the trials of an ordinary Missouri family at the turn of the century. When filming began, Judy Garland played all her scenes tongue in cheek, until Vincente Minnelli explained that it would really only work if she played it straight. (Four years later, in 1948, she had her own way opposite Gene Kelly in *The Pirate*, in which the two of them performed with such high camp that, as Minnelli predicted, it was too hammy for audiences to swallow. The film flopped.) But there remains in *Meet Me in St Louis* an edge to her performance, a raised eyebrow that suggests the very concept of 'ordinariness' depicted in films like these is itself an act of some kind.

In 1936, Dorothy Parker co-wrote a film script called *A Star is Born* which was made into a film, the following year, starring Janet Gaynor and Fredric March. It told the story of Norman Maine, a movie star who falls in love with a woman called Esther, just as her acting career is taking off and his is beginning to sink under the weight of his alcoholism. Maine spirals into despair and the daily rebuke of his wife's success so unhinges him that at the end of the film he walks clean into the sea. In 1954 it was remade as a musical, with James Mason and Judy Garland as the leads.

Despite being a love story, *A Star is Born* is savagely unromantic.

In one key scene, as Esther is being made up in her dressing room, she makes a speech about how she swallowed all the romantic clichés peddled by exactly the kind of film she is shooting at the time, a musical, and look where it got her. 'Love isn't enough,' she says. 'I thought it was.' She looks bitterly amused. 'I thought I was the answer for Norman.' And then she rails against his broken promises, the waiting and waiting and eventual disappointment, when he falls off the wagon each time. 'I hate him for failing!' she says. 'And I hate me too.'

A Star is Born is the musical at its most sophisticated and self-critical. Whenever a particularly tragic exchange is taking place between Esther and Norman, a billboard advertising a dappy musical called *Happiness Ahead* heaves into view. After her outburst in the dressing room, Esther goes out to shoot a jolly number called 'Go And Get Your Long Face Lost', which she performs with the sort of hysterical good cheer that is always a camouflage for misery.

Norman Maine's decision to drown himself rather than live with the indignity of a more successful wife is either an indictment of a culture that fears talented women or an attempt to frighten them into submission – the former, I think, since everything in the film encourages one to identify with her: Norman fails as an American – he gives up! – whereas Esther battles on. At one stage he is offered a small comeback part in a movie but his pride is too big to accept anything short of the lead. The film would rather kill him off than have Esther sacrifice her career for him.

There is a whole sub-category of musicals like this, in which, unusually for the time, successful women marry less successful men who have breakdowns because of it. In *Funny Girl*, Barbra Streisand as Fanny Brice wows Broadway while her husband, played by Omar Sharif, runs up gambling debts and an inferiority complex. After one particularly big loss, she tries to comfort him by saying, 'Everyone has a run of bad luck now and then.'

'How would you know, darling?' he replies bitterly. 'You never lose.'

In *Love Me or Leave Me*, a poor woman's *A Star is Born*, it's James Cagney, the loser-ish, big-talking impresario who gets the same treatment from his superstar wife, Doris Day. In each instance the women end up alone at the end of the picture; even Mary Poppins, God love her, disappears into the sky, alone despite her excellent powers.

There is only one thing a self-respecting heroine in this situation can do. It breaks down into four key stages.

One

A torch song should open with the singer looking wistful, as if remembering the good times, perhaps in the form of a private joke that became a motif of the early days of the relationship and then, when it ceased to amuse and grew actively to annoy, acted as a sort of barometer for its descent into sourness. If the singer concentrates very hard she can just about recapture the feelings she had when she first met the person who would ruin her life, but not without tilting her head to one side, as bad memories bunch on the horizon, waiting to break.

Two

Stage two and the wistfulness of stage one starts to tip into bitterness. The singer comes to her senses and realizes that if she isn't to go mad, she must hold out against sentiment or regret. She tries to strengthen her resolve by bringing to mind all her ex's small failures. Any lingering nostalgia evaporates as the roll call of disappointments lengthens and a massive fury starts working its way towards the surface.

Three

Things come off the rails at stage three, when the immense private hurt she's been nursing bursts out and causes the singer to look at the audience with loathing: fools, what do they know? (She may bang her fist on the table at this point.) The scale of her misery is such that if the singer is serious about expressing it, she will allow herself to slide, momentarily, out of tune. And so, with a howl and a violent sweep of the head, she will get to the crux of the matter: that despite efforts to convince herself otherwise, she still loves the bastard and there is nothing, nothing she can do about it.

Four

There are two possible resolutions: to cut the lights and end on a scream. Or to boil away to wistfulness in its second, deadlier stage: despair.

To carry off a torch song a singer has to have an element of vulnerability about her, a whiff of nervous breakdown. Doris Day has a crack at it at the end of *Love Me or Leave Me*, but she is too solid to be convincing; there she stands, the abandoned woman, with her feet so firmly planted and her back so poker straight that it looks as if the horse has just bolted from under her. She belts out 'Ten Cents a Dance' and sounds suitably stricken, but you don't for a moment believe she's going to break.

For singers who can get it right, the effect on audiences is so gratifying that they can't resist giving the torch treatment to every song that comes along. Streisand's rendition of 'I've Got No Strings', from *Pinocchio*, despite containing the very un-torch-like phrase 'hi-ho-the-merrio', comes out like a declaration of war.

Charity Hope Valentine wasn't beautiful. Her lipstick was too red – it clashed with her hair – her earrings were too big, her dress was too short and she was spun out and dishevelled, the sort of girl who is always to hand when a bus flies through a puddle. She was caught, as her friends put it, in the fly paper of life, which like the bus stop of fear and the rubber glove of destiny, is the circumstance of feeling big feelings in small, shabby environments; her defeats were of the kind that could only be alleviated by gaudiness. If you can't be good, she figured, be gaudy.

The film she was in wasn't even that great. *Sweet Charity* lurched from one unlikely plot device to another, from her being pushed into Central Park lake to getting stuck in a lift with her future fiancé, to the couple's arbitrary attendance of a 'flower power' church service, to facilitate a cameo by Sammy Davis Jr. Although she was played by

Shirley MacLaine at her most winsome, this was no *Cabaret*, and she no Sally Bowles.

Charity worked in a dance hall as a hostess, which in the late '60s meant that she was not the kind of girl men married, at least not in a conservative genre like the movie musical. Despite this unpromising set-up, somewhere in the middle of the film something happened. Something, in the language of the musical, wonderful. An Italian matinee idol invited Charity to his penthouse. (They met, naturally, after a collision in the street.) 'You make life fun for me,' he said, on the strength of one evening out, and, excusing himself for a moment, left Charity to look around his million-dollar gaff.

For a space of some ten minutes, Charity toured the apartment with all the wonder and regret of one suddenly confronted by her own dismal place in the world. She turned the chandelier on and off; she counted the suits in Vittorio's wardrobe; she ran a finger across the surface of his opulent life until tears came to her eyes and shoulders drooping, toes pointing inwards, she blinked up at the camera and croaked out a song called 'If My Friends Could See Me Now'. As she sang she began to caper around the room, mimicking the frenzied efforts of so many performers before her – Groucho Marx, Al Jolson, Fred Astaire – taking great, manic-depressive swings at the good times while the spotlight held the bad ones at bay.

Sweet Charity came out in 1968 when the musical was all but dead and *Hello, Dolly!* about to deliver the final blow. Still, when Charity Hope Valentine dives on the bed, hurls herself on the furniture, works up to a big, top hat waving, '60s beads swinging climax – 'they'd never believe it' – summit gained – 'they'd never believe it' – mood lifted – 'they'd never believe it' – fears conquered! – 'they'd never believe it!' – it's that same rendition of the world in all its hope and outrage that the musical captured at the height of its glory. The lights go out and her voice instantly minimizes. (The voice always minimizes.) 'If my friends. Could. See. Me.' Her eyes fill with tears. 'Now?'

Grubby Girl Makes Good, Sings! 'Hey girls, look. It's me!'

By the time *Sweet Charity* was made, things were starting to look up for talented women in the musical. They were still required to be alone at the end of the film; but unlike their predecessors they were at least allowed to be happy about it.

Bob Fosse shot two endings to *Sweet Charity*. In one, Charity and Oscar, the uptight fiancé who dumped her for being too unconventional, get back together (or rather, he forgives her for having slept with other men and she's just so *grateful* that she overlooks the fact he's been a complete bastard to her up until then). In the second ending, after spending a night of misery on a bench in Central Park, Charity shrugs off Oscar and is shown in the closing scene to be striding through Manhattan in the sunlight, happy as a lark. Fosse used the second ending.

Sondheim: An Interlude

What Would Barbra Do?

When I was a student, I remember coming out of the English faculty one day and overhearing someone say, '... of course, Terry hasn't said anything sensible about Marxism for twenty years.' I thought it the most sophisticated thing I had ever heard and longed for an excuse to repeat it, preferably at a dinner party, where the other guests would laugh as if it was the wittiest take on Terry they had ever heard. Sondheim's musicals are that kind of party and only certain guests are invited.

After graduation it didn't take me long to discover that dinner parties at which everyone sits around labouring to say witty things are the ones at which no one enjoys themselves. Much, I thought, like a Sondheim musical. I tried with him, I really did. I bought the soundtrack to *Company* and I liked the odd individual Sondheim number: 'I'm Still Here', from *Follies*, in which the old broad gets to bawl aggressively at the audience about how, what with everything she's been through, it's a miracle she's still around; and of course, 'Send in the Clowns', from *A Little Night Music*. But Sondheim hadn't been on my radar, growing up – my mother thought him uptight and a show-off – and coming to it in adulthood, I found all those smart, cynical characters with the warmth squeezed out of them, all those references to Mahler, just too self-satisfied to enjoy.

Then I saw a production in London of *Sunday in the Park with George*. It was kind of cool, the way the guy, Seurat, was slated by his contemporaries but turned out to be a bigger genius than all of them, obviously a riposte by Sondheim to his own critics. I was surprised by how funny it was and how passionate. I looked Sondheim up on Wikipedia. Did you know that he was an ace creator of cryptic crosswords? And that, after the failure of yet another of his shows, he considered throwing in the towel and going into another line of work, like writing pulp fiction?

I was humming the theme from *Sunday in the Park with George* the day afterwards and looked to see if they had it on iTunes (they did; but only some pissy 'tribute' version sung by a choir in the Albert Hall). I listened to the *Company* album again. There was a song called 'The Ladies Who Lunch' which had a line in it about buying a hat that ended with the afterthought, 'Does anyone still wear a hat?' It was one of those lines that I had considered too cute and self-satisfied, too much a celebration of the clever, tinkly people at the dinner party. But after repeated play, it started to sound more wistful. When Elaine Stritch croaks, 'Does anyone still wear a hat?' the feeling you get is of someone calling time on her own usefulness.

There's a song about a hat in *Sunday in the Park with George*. Seurat obsesses about getting the hat in his painting right. I suppose a hat is as good a unit of reality as anything. I interviewed Muriel Spark once at her house in Tuscany and she told me the story of how her bag had been stolen from the back of her chair, in Rome. When the Italian policeman asked her what had been in the bag, she said, 'A poem.'

'Can you describe the poem?' he said. (Italian policemen, she explained, always understood the existential dimension.)

She told him: 'It was about a hat.'

I am definitely coming round to Sondheim.

Title Song

Title Song

There is an excellent newsletter put out by Smash, the Guildford-based Stage Musical Appreciation Society, called *Spotlight on Musicals*, which when it reviews a show also offers informal advice about how much experience of musicals you need to enjoy it. So, for example, a revival in Winchester of *A Chorus Line* might be recommended for a general audience, whereas a performance of early Kurt Weill might be judged suitable only for those with a well-advanced interest. Sondheim's *Pacific Overtures* would be strongly discouraged for novices.

There is one musical that, were it ever to enjoy a revival on stage, Smash would have to issue a code red about; a musical that makes *Pacific Overtures* look like *Mary Poppins*. It is the Everest, the *Finnegans Wake*, the black belt of the genre, the one in which eighty years of film and theatrical tradition boil away to just one, terrifying word: *Yentl*. I first came across *Yentl* when, at the age of fifteen, some friends and I skipped an RE class and were detained in a classroom over lunch. The woman in charge was a supply teacher and I don't recall seeing her again after that day, which, in light of what happened, makes me think she might have been an impostor, like those people who wander into hospitals in a rented white coat and start 'treating' the sick.

The classroom was hot. It was one of the few in school still furnished with wooden flip-top desks and, in warm weather, the gashes in the surface gave off a smell like rotting logs. 'Wait here,' said the teacher, and disappeared. Five minutes later there was a rumble in the corridor and she reappeared towing the old telly from the science block. 'Somebody draw the blinds,' she said.

What Would Barbra Do?

Oh, God. We looked at each other. What was this? *Songs of Praise*? Harry Secombe's *Take the High Road*? Please, mercy, not the Open University's religious studies programming. She said: next time we were tempted to be cavalier about the resources at our disposal we were to think about those less fortunate than ourselves. And with an eerie smile she swivelled round to locate the video channel.

For the first few moments it was too dark to see anything. Then the words '1904, Eastern Europe' flashed across the screen and a village materialized out of the gloom. An old book peddler pushed his cart across the square. 'Picture books for women, sacred books for men!' he called. The camera cut to a group of women discussing cabbages and then to a group of men discussing Genesis. One of the women broke away from the cabbage stall and sidled up to the book cart, where she started leafing through a sacred text. The peddler chuckled and said there, there, dear, you've got the wrong pile, women don't read sacred books! Oh, God. Women and religion. This was going to be worse than we thought.

The action bumped along for a while; the woman didn't want to get married; she wanted to study. Her father died. Our heads lolled on the desks; dust motes danced in the sunlight. In the background, tinkly piano music started. As dusk gathered, the woman wrapped a prayer shawl round her shoulders and the piano music intensified and was joined by violins. We raised our heads. As her singing gathered force it started to become clear that, in descending order of offensive elements, what we were dealing with here was:

Barbra Streisand
Playing a nineteenth-century Polish woman who, in order to
Study the bible
Disguises herself as a man
While singing in a style that can only be described as
Rabbinical.

While the others tried to saw open their wrists with the blunt edge of a ruler I sighed and, predictably, heart-sinkingly, resigned myself to the fact that I would probably quite enjoy it.

Forty-five minutes later, before the film had finished, the bell rang and we flew out of the door as one might through an emergency exit opened at 35,000 feet. There were so many unanswered questions. What lay in store for Yentl? Would sexist nineteenth-century Polish society prevent her from realizing her dream? Would her story analogize with the problems facing modern-day women? Would anyone other than Streisand be allowed to sing? It would be years before I saw the end of the film, in very different circumstances, and would get to find out.

Ah, Babs. How to explain? She didn't have a nose job, she didn't change her name; whatever errors of judgement she made in *Hello, Dolly!* it was these two things, said my mother, that mattered about Babs and were why Babs mattered. She saw *Funny Girl* in 1968 when it first came out in the cinema and the experience had never left her. There were gasps, she said, during the opening scene when Streisand walked down the corridor of the New Amsterdam theatre and turned sideways to look in the mirror. My mother was with her friend Sylvia that day and she was still going on about it thirty years later. This was the first time, she said, that a woman was allowed to be visible without being beautiful and that meant blonde, with a small nose and no antecedents in Eastern Europe. More than anything put out there by Betty Friedan or Marilyn French or Gloria Steinem the image of feminism for Sylvia and my mum was Barbra Streisand's nose in profile and her collection that year of an Oscar for it, in a see-through sequined jumpsuit that the wardrobe department on *Valley of the Dolls* would've written off as too camp. That was style, they said. That was performance.

When people think of her these days, it's more often as Mecha-Streisand, the giant, killer robot from *South Park* who plots to take over the world from her mountain condo. Mecha-Streisand spends half her time hollering show tunes and the other half rampaging through towns, picking up tower blocks and shaking people out of them to their deaths. It's a kind of surrealist tribute to that moment in the concert when she duets with herself and which she followed up seven years later in Vegas by *trio-ing* with herself (a small, live child was brought on to play the Young Babs, singing alongside the Adult Babs and the giant projected playback of Babs), creating a vortex of ever-decreasing circles of Babs, which if they could have figured out how to harness the energy from would probably have split the atom.

You can either read this egotism as a feminist retort to sexism in the entertainment business or as the equality-in-monstrosity argument used by female gang members: if men can be bad, women can be worse.

I first saw *Funny Girl* in my teens and loved it. It is an old-fashioned triumph-of-the-underdog type story from the era when Babs could still laugh at herself, before *The Mirror Has Two Faces* or her duet with Bryan Adams. It's a savage film that ends on a shriek and she just tears up the screen. Go Babs, I thought. You rule. To me, it was the musicals equivalent of a Smiths album and I watched it again and again. Over the years, as my Babs-worship grew, so too did my radar for Babs-haters. They are everywhere. Some of them hate her because she is loud, some because she is a woman, some because she is Jewish and some because she is a Democrat. (OK, so maybe a few of them don't like her because she has made the odd bad film and record.) Some hate her because her efforts on behalf of the Democrats could conceivably recruit for Republicanism.

I think it is safe to say that if Isaac Bashevis Singer had been alive on 31 December 1999, he probably wouldn't have been seeing in the millennium at the MGM Grand in Las Vegas. The Nobel prize winning author of eighteen novels and twenty collections of short stories, including 'The Spinoza of Market Street' and 'A Friend of Kafka', had, in an article written for the *New York Times* some years earlier, blamed the woman performing on stage that night for one of the greatest crimes against literature of the twentieth century. The victim was his own work. The violence done to it was Barbra Streisand.

In 1962 Singer wrote a short story called 'Yentl the Yeshiva Boy'. It was about the daughter of a rabbi in nineteenth-century Eastern Europe who wished, in defiance of Talmudic law, to go to university. And so after her father died, she disguised herself as a man, took to the road and via a complicated chain of events ended up married to the ex-fiancée of the man she was in love with. You can see why it appealed to Streisand; Judaism, feminism, the pursuit of a dream in the face of opposition – all it needed was some songs and it had everything a good musical requires. In 1974 *Yentl* was turned into a stage play and in 1983 it was made into a film musical.

It probably didn't help Singer's opinion of the end result that his own contributions to the script were rejected. Streisand thought that, er, there was another writer who could do the material more justice: her. She collaborated with Jack Rosenthal on the script. The score was by her old friends Alan and Marilyn Bergman, who had written some of her biggest hits including 'The Way We Were' and 'You Don't Bring Me Flowers', and Streisand also elected to produce and direct the film. The way she saw it, the only way the songs would work was if they were used to give voice to Yentl's thoughts, as a woman, compared to her outward actions, as a man. This meant that Streisand, who was to play Yentl, would have to sing all the songs herself. Yes, all of them.

If my tone sounds mocking then it is affectionately so. One feels protective of *Yentl*, as of all things that are heartfelt and at the same time disastrous. Singer's response to the film in the *New York Times* was slightly less appreciative. It started mildly, as all great explosions do, with the observation that it was funny, he had never imagined Yentl singing songs. The songs in the film, he added, seemed to come 'from all sides'. It was also interesting, he observed, how in the version of the script he had turned in, Yentl wasn't present in every scene. Beginning to rev up, he suggested that Streisand was 'exceedingly kind' to herself, that she did not allow anyone else to showcase their talents and that the sheer, overbearing force of her presence throughout the film ensured that 'poor Yentl', as he put it, was absent.

This was just the warm-up. Over the course of another five hundred or so words, Singer rained fire down on Streisand and what she had done to his story.

At the end of the film, Yentl gets on a boat and sails to America, singing all the way, whereas in the original story she stays in Poland. Drawing himself up to his full, Nobel prize winning height, Singer compared this alteration to a scriptwriter deciding that Madame Bovary should wind up taking a cruise along the Riviera, or that Anna Karenina should marry an American millionaire instead of committing suicide, or that Dostoevsky's Raskolnikov should become a Wall Street broker instead of going to Siberia.

'This is what Miss Streisand did by making Yentl, whose greatest passion was the Torah, go on a ship to America, singing at the top of her lungs.' There was more acid in his use of the word 'Miss' in this sentence than in any other word in the review. He continued: 'Why would she decide to go to America? Weren't there enough yeshivas in Poland or in Lithuania where she could continue to study? Was going to America Miss Streisand's idea of a happy ending for Yentl? What would Yentl have done in America? Worked in a sweatshop twelve hours a day where there is no time for learning? Would she try to marry a salesman in New York, move to the Bronx or to Brooklyn and rent an apartment with an icebox and a dumbwaiter? This kitsch ending summarizes all the faults of the adaptation. It was done without any kinship to Yentl's character, her ideals, her sacrifice, her great passion for spiritual achievement. As it is, the whole splashy production has nothing but a commercial value.'

One has sympathy for Singer inasmuch as he was denied the consolation of huge royalties and the bringing of his work to a wider audience; for that, the film needed to have played better with people who weren't already Babs fans. But writers are always throwing hissy fits about the damage done to their work by Hollywood; if they don't like it, they shouldn't sell the rights. And Streisand was right about one thing: her ending made perfect sense in the context. If Singer had been conversant with the ways of the movie musical, he would have realized that there was something very specific Yentl could have done in America, something that Streisand clearly nodded towards in that final scene on the boat, which was an echo of a scene from *Funny Girl*. To be the heroine of a musical you have to be upwardly mobile and, as Streisand's Yentl found out, there's only so far a girl can go in a nineteenth-century Polish village. After docking in New York Yentl would, of course, have ditched religion and found work in the back row of a lousy cabaret act, whence she would have been discovered, a remarkable singer, actress and comedienne, and made the star of a Broadway show. In no time at all she would have had the world at her feet.

*

Ten years after I first saw *Yentl* I saw it again, of my own free will this time, at a Yentl and Lentil evening. A Yentl and Lentil evening sounds like the sort of thing you would only do to write about afterwards, but it actually exists, in the real world, as a semi-regular event held at the flat of whichever of my friends who likes the film has the biggest telly. Since there are only two of us in this category, and since I have a rubbish telly, it is always at Adi's house. There are no set dates; you just sort of know when the time is right for another one. The lentil element came about at the suggestion of a friend of Adi's who is a newspaper sub and to whom these things come naturally. I only wish I could say that 'lentil' was the name of a hallucinogenic drug; but no, they really are small, flat pulses in a sauce of some description which we pop while singing along to 'Papa Can You Hear Me'.

Until it came out on DVD recently the only copy of the film in our possession was an ancient VHS recording made from BBC2 in the era when Richard Baker still read the news. It came to light one day when I threw a tape in the machine to record *Casualty* and – 'Jesus, what's that?' said my flatmate – a woman was sailing under the Statue of Liberty, howling. 'Oh my God, it's *Yentl*!' I took the fact of its survival as strong proof that God likes show tunes and after the inaugural viewing it became a part of our lives.

It's hard to explain the appeal of *Yentl*. Although it distils all the best, or worst, depending on your viewpoint, excesses of the musical, it doesn't look much like one. There are no colourful costumes or beautiful set designs or big numbers with people parading through the streets banging kettledrums. There is no spectacle. It's all brown and muddy and poorly lit. Bits of it are intentionally funny, like when Yentl is being measured for a wedding suit and tries to hide from the tailor's prying eyes and the tailor says, 'A tailor's like a doctor, what's to be ashamed?' And bits of it are unintentionally funny, like when Mandy Patinkin goes swimming naked in the lake and the light is all golden and you can see the water hanging in droplets from his beard and it looks like a 1970s porn movie.

Yentl came out the same year as *Jaws III*, *Octopussy* and *Return of the Jedi*. No one could spell its title, let alone pronounce it. It was so perversely unfashionable that among existing Babs fans it became an instant classic. Only Babs could have the genius to put out something like this in 1983! There were two other gender swap films that came out around then, Dustin Hoffman's *Tootsie* and *Mr. Mom*, a comedy starring Michael Keaton in which the mom went to work and, hilarity, the dad stayed at home to be a house-husband. Both of them made the top ten and Hoffman got the Oscar for *Tootsie*. Although it wasn't a flop, *Yentl* was not a big box office success and was the target of some satire, which one assumes Streisand took as confirmation of its integrity.

The *Yentl* score plays more like a concept album than a soundtrack, what with there being only one voice on it, and you can't really appreciate the complexity of the arrangements until you have tried to sing them in karaoke. It might surprise you to learn that most of the *Yentl* soundtrack, including 'Papa Can You Hear Me', exists on the play list of at least one London karaoke bar; it certainly surprised the rest of our group when we ordered and performed it.

Over the years, the sound quality on the tape-of-destiny, as my *Yentl* video became known, has eroded and to hear anything you have to turn the volume up to maximum setting, which muffles the voices and makes the plant on top of the TV shake, especially during 'Piece of Sky', in which Babs sings about how she wants more than she's got and what's wrong with that, although, in the context of a film that she directed, produced, co-wrote, starred in and in which she sang all the songs, you wonder what more she wanted: to be the scenery? Mandy Patinkin plays Avigdor, the man she falls in love with and who in real life has a Tony award and over ten albums of mainly Broadway songs to his name, which may account for why he spends so much of the film frowning. (Likewise in *Funny Girl*, Omar Sharif had a single solo which – 'Ahem, may I make a little suggestion?' – Streisand thought might work better as a duet.) Amy Irving gets to hum a tune at one point, but Babs talks over it.

'Do you think when Patinkin signed up he thought he was going to get to sing?' asks Adi, every time we watch it.

'I think the word "musical" probably raised his hopes, yes.'

We felt so sorry for Patinkin that as a gesture of support we went to see his performance in the kids' film *Elmo in Grouchland*.

'I always burn my baked apples,' Adi never fails to sigh, during the scene in which Amy Irving burns her baked apples and Yentl tells her they are better that way.

'Since when do you bake apples?' I say.

'Oh!' she screams. 'This is the bit with the tree with the brother Anshel!'

What Would Barbra Do?

*

I was in New York for a few days seeing a friend recently and he suggested, one evening, that we go for a drink at the top of the Beekman Tower.

'As in Beekman Place?' I said.

'What?' he said.

'As in, "Did you have to go back to Beekman Place?"'

'I have no idea what you're talking about.'

We rode the elevator to the twenty-sixth floor and looked out over the East river to the Pepsi Cola sign, down First Avenue past the Trump Tower and towards the UN building with the limousines parked outside. They pipe music onto the terrace of the Beekman, so you can drink your raspberry martini to Motown's greatest hits and '80s soul and – they know their customers – the title song to *The Way We Were*.

'You see?' I said, as the bells rang in the opening bars and the strings began to swell.

He sighed. 'This is a Barbra Streisand thing, isn't it. No; I don't see.'

That night on the terrace I tried to put Babs's reputation into the context of her early failures and to explain how her films endlessly worried at the scab of not being good enough. I tried to explain how people who succeed in the face of opposition like this develop a self-regard so aggressive that, long after victory has been secured, it still characterizes everything they do. In *The Way We Were*, Streisand's character always suspects Robert Redford's of thinking he's too good for her, because he is blond and all-American and she has funny hair and square shoes and spends her time talking about Lenin, while all he wants to do is hang out with his Waspy friends at their neutrally decorated apartment on Beekman Place and make jokes about the Roosevelts. His friends are all socialites and ex-sorority girls who sniggered at Streisand's character in college and then, years later, when she and Redford have moved to California so he can become a screenwriter, she discovers he's having an affair with a girl he used to date at college and it seems to her less like an infidelity than an indictment of her entire being and, confronting him, she says that she doesn't give a damn about the affair but, 'Did you have to go back to Beekman Place?'

There was a pause after I made this speech. My friend looked at me, then threw *The Prince of Tides* in my face. I sighed. 'You don't understand anything.'

I once met a guy who knew a guy who'd been at school with a woman named Marjorie Gubernickel, who apparently worked for the Barbra Streisand Foundation. That's as close as I have ever got to the real Babs. I did however meet the world's foremost Streisand impersonator, Steven Brinberg, after seeing him perform once at the Jermyn Street Theatre. Despite the wig, nails and eyelashes, it isn't accurate to call what Steve does a drag act. He doesn't lip-synch, he sings, in a pitch-perfect falsetto, and although his routine satirizes Streisand's excesses with knife-like acuity, he is, as he puts it breathlessly, 'never cruel'. His performance of 'You Don't Bring Me Flowers' in which he sings both the Babs and Neil Diamond parts is something to behold. For the last thirteen years, Steve's full time job has been as Barbra Streisand. Now, I'm a big Babs fan. But even I find this a little hard to get my head around.

When we meet, he's in London to perform in the bar beneath the Prince of Wales Theatre, a late night venue that opens for cabaret after *Mamma Mia* has finished in the auditorium above. To Steve's excitement, it was here that the stage production of *Funny Girl* played in the 1960s; it's the first time he has performed in the same venue as his idol. At 11 p.m. the room is packed, mostly with older gay men, but also with a few husband and wife types and groups of giggling girls. Steve has expanded his act to include impressions of Maggie Smith, Judi Dench, Carol Channing and others and it's halfway through his Katharine Hepburn routine that the elderly couple in the row in front of me seem to clock that this isn't the real Streisand and leave in a fury. 'Yeah,' says Steve. 'That sometimes happens. I think it was in a casino in Connecticut where some people said after the show, wow, that was amazing, I can't believe it was so reasonably priced. How can she make any money in a place this small?'

The next day we meet outside *Mary Poppins* on Old Compton Street. I am worried I won't recognize him as a man, but there he is, in a leather jacket and his own hair, looking smaller than he did on stage and smiling ruefully. 'Hi,' he says and we walk to Patisserie Valerie for tea.

'It's less of an act than a way of life,' says Steve. 'I think the possibilities are endless, just because *she's* endless. I probably haven't sung "People" more than her because she did *Funny Girl* on stage for two years, but I'm sure I've sung "Evergreen" more times and it was kind of freaking me out last night cos I thought, this is almost the first time I've been singing songs that she sang in the same building, except I did sing "People" at the Kennedy Center the first time with Marvin [Hamlisch, Streisand's musical director, with whom Steve has himself collaborated], and she sang that there in a special in '75.'

Steve knows a lot about Barbra Streisand. He knows that there are forty-five missing minutes of footage slashed from *On A Clear Day*, the Streisand/Yves Montand musical, and that they have never been found; he knows the names of the songs her sister has recorded; he knows that her son lives somewhere near him in the Bronx because he sees him on the subway sometimes – although he's never felt brave enough to go up to him; he wouldn't want to intrude. Steve worships Babs the way some men worship Manchester United, only when he puts on his wig and eyelashes, it's as if he is actually given the chance to play.

He grew up in New York and both his parents loved musicals. In another life, he says, his father would have gone into show business instead of working as a salesman. Steve discovered his talent when he was still at school. 'The voice,' he says, and sighs. 'Well, I've always been able to do voices.' As a boy he would sing along to his father's Broadway soundtracks, only he would try to sound like the person who was singing. He did Shirley MacLaine and Julie Andrews before he found a natural home for his voice with Streisand. 'I put it all down on a tape one day and my dad found it. And he said, I found this tape, it has your name on it but it's Barbra Streisand. I said, Dad, that's me.'

What Would Barbra Do?

Wow. He didn't freak out?

'No, no.'

Because some dads would freak out at that.

'No. He loved it.'

Steve played the tape to his friends. Of all the impressions, they said, the strongest was of Streisand. Someone suggested that he try to put a show together. 'I looked in the mirror, I didn't exactly see Barbra. But they kept saying that the voice is so good.' He did a few numbers at a club in New York called Don't Tell Mama, some as Streisand, some as himself. (The nearest his audience gets to hearing his regular voice these days is when he does Cher.)

The shows went down so well that he scheduled a few more and was initially torn over whether to concentrate on Julie Andrews, Cher or Babs. Andrews and Cher were problematic, he says, because the fact that they already laugh at themselves reduces the comedy potential of his act. This wasn't a problem with Streisand.

Steve's father was injured in a car crash and had to give up his job in sales, at which point his mother went to work in a gift shop. His parents eventually bought the shop and ran it together.

'They had signed pictures of all the stars in there,' says Steve, 'and, of course, all the pictures from my shows on display.' As they got older and less mobile, whenever a new show opened on Broadway, Steve would go to see it first, to make sure it was worth a trip for them. The last show they all saw together was Julie Andrews in *Victor/Victoria*.

Steve finds it a bit passé to link the appreciation gay men have for Streisand with the theory that, by virtue of her unconventional looks and attitude, she was herself excluded from the mainstream and so understands what they've been through. 'I mean, sure, whatever,' says Steve. 'People say she's identified with the struggle and everything, but it's really more to do with talent. You know? You're not going to see thousands of gay men lining up to buy tickets for . . . Jennifer Lopez. It's talent. The Voice. I mean I love Julie and Liza very very much. Liza is my number two. She came to my show, I was *thrilled*.'

Steve wouldn't even classify himself as the most hardcore Babs fan out there. 'Ohmygod, there are *some* people who . . . put it this way, if she had a car accident and hit two children, her fans would say well they must have provoked her.' He rolls his eyes. 'Absolute blind adoration.' Steve thinks it would be fairer to the fans if, when Babs staged a concert, the organizers set up a phone line you could ring to answer Babs-related trivia questions – 'the higher you score, the closer you get to sit.' In any case, he's not such a fan of the concerts, which he thinks are too big and expensive. He can't understand why she never did another Broadway show after *Funny Girl*. 'She did *Funny Girl* from January of '64 in Philadelphia to the end of 1965. That's eight shows a week, six songs and then there were reports that she would skip some of the songs –'

Yeah. I heard that too.

'– which surprises me because I think that as a perfectionist she would never give less than her all. I know I never have. '

Rather than stage a concert, Steve would prefer her to make another film or do a cameo in a sitcom. He's heard she's a fan of *Desperate Housewives*. 'It just seems such a waste, when you could do the slightest thing and it would give so many people pleasure. One little cameo, would it kill her?'

If we're being honest, I say, I think we have to admit at this point that Streisand has made some terrible films and recorded some terrible music. I'm thinking in particular of the 1981 disaster, *All Night Long*, with Gene Hackman and all those limp Carole King covers in the '70s. I mention the six-disc boxed set, at least a third of which is unplayable, and Steve looks immensely sad. 'Well, there was better stuff that was left out. There were all sorts of singles. I don't know. I guess it was just what she wanted to put on there. Everyone has their own opinion.' He gives a hollow laugh.

What fascinates me about Steve is the diversity of his audience. He has performed across America to naturally receptive audiences on the east and west coasts, and to less obviously sympathetic crowds in Texas and the Midwest. I can't imagine how Steve goes down in the south. He says he's been confronted a couple of times. 'One woman said, oh, you're mocking the greatest talent of all time! Your singing is great but you shouldn't speak. Don't say anything. I said, you gotta be kidding. I'm so careful not to say anything that would be unkind, because that's not me.'

That wasn't the kind of hassle I had in mind. Hasn't there ever been homophobia? Well, says Steve, the first time he played in Idaho he was a little nervous. But he says audiences were just grateful he showed up; the real stars, they told him afterwards, would never stoop so low as to trek out to their neck of the woods. They were only too happy to receive an impersonator, even if he was a guy. 'The only bad responses I get sometimes are from some Jewish groups. When I try to make a booking with them they'll say, oh, we've never had anything like thaaaat. And I say, I'm a nice Jewish boy playing a nice Jewish girl, what could be more natural?' He has also been criticized by gay groups, he says, who 'hate all kinds of drag shows because they think it's a step back in the movement. Or worse, they think that it's going to be too nice. And not political enough. And so I got turned down for a gay cruise for example, and I was like, you've got to be kidding.'

Generally his audiences are divided, like the real Streisand's, between 'seniors – you know, the establishment' and gay men. When he performed recently for a room of Republican mayors at a conference in upstate New York, he brought the house down. 'I don't happen to support the Republicans,' he purred from the stage, 'but who else can afford my tickets?'

Steve was in Los Angeles recently and got a tip-off that the day before, Streisand and Barry Manilow had been seen at a Mexican restaurant in Palm Springs. He is not, of course, the kind of fan who goes tearing off in search of an actual sighting. He is the kind of fan who in his own good time will go to the restaurant the following week to experience the same reality as Barbra and Barry. It's an existential thing: 'It was such a small restaurant,' he says. 'And the waiter said she was very nice. She took a doggy bag home.'

The closest he's actually got to Streisand is a recording of an answer machine message she left on the phone of her friend Tovah

Feldshuh, the actress who played Yentl in the non-musical stage version of which Bashevis Singer so approved. Feldshuh is also a friend of Steve's. 'So she surprised me on my birthday and said this is for you and it was a message that Barbra left her. All it said was, "Hi Tovah, it's Barbra. I just wanted to tell you that Jim and I really loved you in that movie *Kissing Jessica Stein*. We thought your performance was big and small at the same time."'

This is so pretentious that I laugh out loud. Steve looks wounded. 'It was a *nice* message,' he says. (It turns out that there is a thriving black market in celebrity answering machine messages. Steve has a big collection, including the most famous in circulation, that of Faye Dunaway going nuts at the operator. 'She's really yelling,' he says. 'She's like, "The idiocy of this is driving me crazy!"' He also has one of Joan Crawford, harvested from the earliest answering machines in the 1970s, which consists of her saying, 'Oh hi there, call me at eleven. No call me at twelve. No call me at four. Bye!' The holy grail of celebrity answer machine messages is Bette Davis, who despite living ten years longer than Crawford has never surfaced on an answering machine. 'Someone must have one of her somewhere saying, you know, "Call me back."')

What would Steve say if he ever got to meet Babs?

'Oh, Gaad. Well, my sort of imaginary thing would be that she would see my show and say this is really wonderful, thank you, but when you do that gesture with your hand you need to do it a little higher. I would probably just selfishly want to tell her all the projects I think she should still do.' Steve has lots of ideas for new Babs projects. He sees them everywhere. 'Like every time I read a story in the paper – for example there was this woman, an old Jewish lady and she died and she was ninety and I thought, this could be a project for Barbra.'

What does he think she should be recording?

'Well, if I were her I'd just do songbooks, like Rosemary Clooney did. Just do Stephen Sondheim; don't worry about what's popular. Back to Broadway, Back to Broadway Once More, Back to Broadway Forever. It's funny, for someone who hasn't appeared on Broadway in forty-two years, she's still completely identified as probably the biggest star to ever have come out of the theatre. Judy Garland was supposed to do *Mame* – she was going to replace Angela Lansbury. She auditioned, but they were too frightened. It was already 1960, so she was a mess. See that's another thing too, I mean Barbra . . . she's never had horrible personal problems. Maybe some people resent that. We're kinder to . . .'

Basket cases?

'Yeah. Because they don't feel sorry for her, they just think she has everything, so much money, so much fame, so much talent.'

Streisand's sister Rosalind came to Steve's show once, in Los Angeles. 'I heard her in the audience, it was the same laugh – uhahuhah – but she has like a chip on her shoulder. I mean I can't imagine. It's a very love/hate relationship. And they're half-siblings, the whole issue there. And it's nine years' age difference. Someone once said to Barbra, why don't you help her? And she said well, I can get her a record contract but I can't get people to buy the records.'

What Would Barbra Do?

*

We get up to leave. On the way out, we talk about why *Hello, Dolly!* is more like a parody than a proper musical and Steve speculates on what happened to those missing forty-five minutes from *On A Clear Day*. He wonders if they might be in Brighton, where some of the filming took place. Several times, he says, he has come close to getting a tape of his show to Streisand, but every time the final courier in the chain has lost his nerve. Steve thinks it's because of the jokes he tells about her husband, James Brolin. 'She's kind of sensitive about Jim,' he sighs. 'I don't think she'd like me calling him a B-movie actor.'

A Brief Encounter With
Mickey Rooney, Jnr

What Would Barbra Do?

Before meeting him, all I know about Michael Rooney Jnr is that his father is former child star Mickey Rooney and that he choreographed one of the best pop videos of the last five years: Kylie Minogue's 'Can't Get You Out of My Head'. He hasn't given many interviews. This one is backstage at the Albery Theatre in central London, where Rooney is choreographing a new musical, *Ducktastic!*. Before we start I confess that I haven't even been able to find out which of his father's seven wives is his mother.

'Oh, don't worry,' he says, waving a hand in a this-happens-all-the-time gesture. Rooney is buffed and bronzed and looks, at forty-three, like he has never knowingly swallowed a toxin. He was born and bred in Los Angeles. 'My mother was Barbara Thomason, number five on his list. She was an aspiring actress. She is no longer with us.'

Oh, I'm sorry.

'Yuh,' he says. 'What happened was – the story is kind of intense: my mother was murdered.'

God. I'm sorry.

'I don't remember a thing. I was about three or four. And my mum and my dad were going through a divorce. My mum was kind of seeing somebody on the side. But then my father and my mother decided to get back together, and the guy my mum was dating wasn't having it. So he took the very gun that my father gave my mother for protection and killed her in our house. Then killed himself. It was a murder suicide.'

There is a stunned silence.

'So. It was very intense.'

Christ.

He sighs. 'We were in the house when it happened. But I don't remember a thing. We were scurried out and told we were going to see the movie *Mary Poppins*. It wasn't like, oh, your mother's dead upstairs.'

Rooney hasn't said this glibly. But his disregard for the inhibitions of interview is extraordinary. All my questions about *Ducktastic!* and its director, Kenneth Branagh, fly out the window. I ask what happened next.

'Well, my father was going through a tough time in the 1960s, so my grandparents adopted us, my mother's parents. It was stable after that.' He says that if he seems adjusted about it (like, 'yeah'), it's because his grandparents lived completely sane and un-showbizzy lives and he had limited contact with his father. 'My grandparents taught me to rake the leaves in the backyard, clean up my room, all that stuff. And we went to regular schools.'

His mother had three other children with Mickey Rooney, and all four of them were brought up by their maternal grandparents. Rooney got into choreography after a school production of *West Side Story* and, after years of training as a dancer, got his first job as an extra on the television series *Fame*. I ask him at what age he found out what happened to his mother.

'I think I was about thirteen or fourteen. That's when I really understood what had happened. For years I thought my grandmother was my mother, because the transition was so smooth. And then my grandmother sat us down and told us why our mother was no longer around. She started showing us pictures of my mother. The way they did it was really good.'

None of Rooney's sisters went into show business. Two are hairdressers, one a dental technician. He has a further five half-siblings from his father's other marriages, one of which was to Ava Gardner ('I know,' he says, rolling his eyes, 'can you believe it?') and didn't produce children.

'Let me see now: all in there's Timmy, Teddy and Mickey Jr. There's Jimmy and Jonelle. Then there's Kelly, Kerry and Kimmy and my father calls me Kyle, so we kind of all match.'

He has his father's full-moon face. Mickey Rooney is now eighty-five and married to his seventh wife, Jan Chamberlain, with whom he has been for twenty-five years. She has 'really calmed him down'. I can't imagine what sort of a father he would be; in popular memory he's always that grinning teenager, threatening to 'put on the show right here'.

Rooney sighs. 'Up until ten years ago, show business was all he talked about. We'd be at the table and I'd say, I love that couch. And he'd say, "Oh, that couch, that reminds me of when I did this movie." He always feels like there's a camera in front of him or a spotlight and he is number one. Less so now.'

This must have been difficult.

'Yeah. There were times when I would dread going over to his house. But he didn't know what else there was to talk about; that was the only life he'd known. You know, my father was shooting two to three musicals at the same time when he was a kid. They were cranking 'em out back then. They used to put stuff in the soup to keep 'em going – everybody says it was cocaine – anyway, it was some kind of upper. But he's a survivor, unlike poor Judy [Garland, with whom he worked].'

Her kids didn't fare so well, I say.

'I know. Thank God I didn't turn out like Liza, right?'

Did Rooney ever talk to his father about his mother's murder?

'He doesn't like talking about it at all. But we've talked a couple of times. He told me that my mother was one of the most wonderful ladies he had ever met, that she was really nice, a caring person, she was wonderful with us and loved us all. At that point, I really needed to hear that.'

In the past three or four years, says Rooney, he and his sisters have been thinking about looking up the press cuttings and police reports from the time of their mother's murder. 'I think I can handle it now,' he says. When I get back to the office, I look it up too; it happened in 1966; her lover's name was Milos Milocevic.

Bloody Elton

'**B**loody Elton.'

We are in a café in Victoria, my dad and I, after seeing a matinee performance of the stage musical *Billy Elliot*.

'People who hate musicals,' I tell him, 'this is what they hate.' This is the comet trail of a rant that started as we left the theatre and took us five blocks north to a café where we are eating breeze block sized chunks of chocolate cake and drinking tea. My dad's glasses have steamed up. 'One minute you've got a naturalistic performance, the next everyone's broken into song and their characters have completely changed. One minute you're a Geordie miner shouting "coal not dole" the next you're singing something that could've been written for Ronan Keating. Those terrible, terrible songs, except for that one about coppers raking in the overtime and putting extensions on their houses and holidaying in Majorca and the one sung by the dad, because he can't really sing and so has to act his way through it rather than clicking into pop star fantasy and when he breaks down you actually believe it. It's like Christopher Plummer said about *The Sound of Music*, there's good sentimentality and bad sentimentality. And this is bad sentimentality. *Bad sentimentality, Elton.* All those images of flying and reaching for the stars and lighting fires, all those lame-ass rhymes – try/fly, part/heart, far/star – and when the actors sing they get this look on their faces like this is my shot, my pop star moment, well it's not therapy it's acting. It's not about *you*, you snivelling stage school brat. When the *Swan Lake* suite comes on you think, thank God for that, the orchestra must be weeping, some real fucking music. Elton, you twat, I always defended you, I liked the early albums, but this is as if you've been told it's a musical and so you've got out all the clichés that you thought were too lame for your pop songs and God, the utter compliancy of the audience: they're pathetic, one hint of tragedy and they're inhaling like glue sniffers cos it's thirty-five quid for the cheap seats so you'd better wring full value out of it, which means getting all teary when Billy sings to his dead mother, "Mummy I was proud to know you", a scene which is done really delicately in the film but with this it's like a tractor driving through it and it's like yes, *we get the point, it's very sad* but the song goes on and on and don't they understand that if you stretch a piece of elastic too far it loses all its tension? It's the piss-lowest piece of sentimental shite I've seen in a long time. Whenever a big ballad is about to happen, a spotlight narrows around Billy Elliot and he gets a stupid look on his face and for the first few bars he tries to keep the Geordie accent but then he gives up and slides into American, it's like Willie Loman after his "you end up worth more dead than alive" speech suddenly breaking into R. Kelly's "I Believe I Can Fly". At least with Lloyd Webber there's a consistency and some memorable tunes. Honestly. It's like being at the fucking panto.'

My dad finishes his cake and looks over the rim of his teacup. 'I enjoyed it,' he says.

I have a problem with new musicals. I also have a problem with having a problem with them. It's bad enough looking backwards all the time without squandering the one chance you have to look forwards, to enjoy what appears to be a revival of the musical, by taking the position that everything made post '71 is useless. I didn't want to be one of those people who watched *Chicago* and said 'well, it's not *Cabaret*, is it', or said Lloyd Webber was for dummies and that the last proper musical was *Fiddler on the Roof* after which nothing until *A Chorus Line* and thank *God*, darling, for Sondheim.

Many of the shows I saw as a child are still running. The West End at the moment doesn't offer much of a retort to the snobs' view that musicals kill theatrical innovation. Twenty years since opening night and they are still flopping about on the barricades at *Les Misérables*; *Cats* finally died at the New London Theatre after twenty-one years, to be replaced, briefly, by a revival of *Joseph and the Amazing Technicolor Dreamcoat* (a friend who saw it said the numbers were so drawn out that 'Bring Me My Coloured Coat' 'seemed to go on for ten hours. You're like, bring him his fucking coat, somebody, please'), while *The Phantom of the Opera* is still going strong after what seems like two hundred years at Her Majesty's on Haymarket. At the Palace, *The Woman in White* came and went as did something called *The Far Pavilions*, at the Shaftesbury Theatre. It was a musical adaptation of M. M. Kaye's thousand-page novel set in nineteenth-century India and you learnt everything you needed to know about it from the blurb on the posters: 'A British Officer, An Indian Princess, Daring to Dream.'

I went to see it just to prove myself right and it was every bit as terrible as expected. The friend I was with got hysterical during a number about Afghanistan ('Afghanist-a-a-an!') and we both had to double over and fish for things in our bags when the hero, in a sudden very loud and tuneless key change, shouted, 'Must we die by the gun / must we die by the sword?' I hadn't laughed so hard since being ambushed by 'Never start to weep / think of Meryl Streep' in the new stage version of *Fame* in '95. That ran for a decade.

The problem with these productions, apart from the bad music, bad scripts, bad acting and bad singing, is their tone, a sort of crazed cheerfulness unique to people who have never allowed a negative thought about themselves to surface. The songs are performed in a style that, in the TV series *Pop Idol*, was used to crush contestants' hopes with a single word: 'cabaret'. Not all cabaret is bad, but bad cabaret is worse than anything, including German reggae. Bad theatrical singers in Britain always perform in a thin, tremulous voice with a terrible American accent and a mad look in the eye – the singular misery of the untalented singer performing songs written for people with talent.

Take the musical *Rent*. It was written by Jonathan Larson and first staged in New York in 1996, where it became a big hit, largely thanks to teenage fans who went back to see it again and again. It is a 'modern-day rendition of *La Bohème*', in which the residents of a squat in New York's Alphabet City struggle with poverty, AIDS, homophobia and bad songwriting; none of the songs match the individual characters, who themselves all seem interchangeable and equally unconvincing. *Rent* aimed for a sort of *Midnight Cowboy* feel, only the people in it looked as if the hardest thing they had ever struggled with was wheat intolerance and fluffing their audition for the Gap ad. It tackled 'issues' with the subtlety and insight of the children's programme *Rainbow* – 'we know a song about AIDS, don't we, Bungle?' 'Yes, Geoffrey, we do.' The moral was that it isn't easy living a bohemian lifestyle, or la vie bohème as they put it, Frenchly, but that you have to follow your heart all the same.

What *Rent* and other musicals like it don't seem to understand is that sincerity is a by-product of some other conviction, not a goal in itself and certainly not a facial expression. We have a natural resistance these days to being inspired, because everything tries to inspire us. Yogurt can change your life, anything with a PR budget can change your life. When all those terrible singers gurn through a song, you can just tell that they're hanging on to the insane hope that maybe, in spite of all evidence to the contrary, this is actually good because good and bad have been exploded as categories in these post-modern times and isn't success just a question of how bad you want it?

Bad musicals fall into three broad categories: the bad/bad musical, the bad/good musical and the good/bad musical. The bad/bad musical is a straightforward commercial and critical failure; the bad/good musical is a commercial success that is actually lousy; and the good/bad musical is a musical that despite being vulnerable to mockery – Neil Diamond's 1980 remake of *The Jazz Singer*, say – is actually, if you can bring yourself to say it, so audaciously bad as to be kind of great, in the traditional manner.

Bad/bad

Let's start with the bad/bad musical, since it's the easiest to get a handle on. Most shows in this category give themselves away in their title. Musical adaptations of the bible have proved very lucrative, but you know instinctively that *Moses, My Love* (off Broadway, 1999) wasn't one of them. You get the same whiff of disaster off *Mutiny!*, a musical by David Essex based on the mutiny on the *Bounty*. Where the use of an exclamation mark in the title was once an expression of joy in a musical, it is these days more of a wink, a sort of begging gesture from the writers not to be taken too seriously, not to judge them too harshly if the silliness doesn't come off. By their very nervousness they ensure that it won't; if they don't believe in their own show, neither will the audience.

The other type of bad/bad musical is the one that believes in itself that bit too much. It is never a good idea to use material the audience is overly familiar with, unless you are very confident of your adaptation. The 1996 musical *Heathcliff* was in trouble before it even opened, mainly because people have an image in their heads of *Wuthering Heights* and it doesn't include Cliff Richard. The lyrics really didn't flatter Tim Rice's abilities relative to Emily Brontë's. There's a vain hope in these kinds of upmarket adaptations that through use of archaic language – 'whence comes my help?', 'whom' for 'who', lots of references to 'quitting this earth' – they will somehow qualify as operatic and force people to respect them. But their pretentiousness only brings them down.

To get an idea of all the different ways in which a musical can flop you only have to look back through the playbill of the Majestic Theatre, a 1,800-seat leviathan on West 44th Street and Broadway, one of New York's most famous venues. Before *The Phantom of the Opera* moved in, the Majestic had only had six big musical hits in its eighty-year history: *Carousel*, *South Pacific*, *The Music Man*, *Camelot*, *Funny Girl* and *Fiddler on the Roof*. The list of flops is much longer and includes works by some of the biggest names in Broadway history.

Bloody Elton

The first came three years after the theatre opened, when *The International Revue*, a hugely expensive production starring Gertrude Lawrence and a Spanish dancer called Argentinita, horrified first night audiences by being so long that the second half didn't start until 11 p.m. In 1933 a musical by George and Ira Gershwin called *Pardon My English* was the pair's biggest flop, largely as a result of bad timing: it was set in Germany and opened just as Hitler was elected, blowing the carefree mood they were aiming for. Later that year, *Strike Me Pink* with Jimmy Durante did solid business but was too insubstantial to stick around for long, as was Bela Lugosi's thriller-musical *Murder at the Vanities*. Big stars were no insurance against failure: in the late 1930s, Durante and Ethel Merman starred in a flaccid musical revue called *Stars in Your Eyes*, directed by *South Pacific*'s Joshua Logan, but this didn't stop it from shutting after four months. Then came *Yokel Boy*, a musical by someone called Lew Brown, about which you learn all you need from the title. Cole Porter's *Mexican Hayride* was the story of a crook who goes on the run from the FBI by employing a number of hilarious disguises, but it didn't fool the audience for a moment; as musical comedy grew more sophisticated, it was no longer adequate for shows just to stitch a loose narrative round a programme of unrelated songs.

And then, finally, *Carousel* opened in 1945 and ran for two years solid, followed by *South Pacific* in '49. In the 1950s there was an uninspiring show called *By the Beautiful Sea*, a romance set in Coney Island at the turn of the century, followed by the phenomenally successful *The Music Man*, and then Lerner and Loewe's *Camelot*, for which Richard Burton won a Tony as King Richard.

What Would Barbra Do?

Mary Martin, star of many a Broadway hit and always, to her chagrin, replaced in the film version, flopped in '63 with *Jennie*, a musical based on the early career of a great dramatic stage actress of the '20s called Laurette Taylor. Martin turned down the starring roles in *Funny Girl* and *Hello, Dolly!* to appear in this. (I discovered just recently that Martin's son is none other than Larry 'JR' Hagman.)

Then came Sondheim's unsuccessful *Anyone Can Whistle*, in which patients from a mental hospital escape into a local community to teach the townsfolk a lesson about the dangers of labelling people; it's . . . it's as if 'mad' people are the only ones who can see through the hypocrisy and contradictions of the 'sane' world. How ironic! *Funny Girl* followed, then *Fiddler on the Roof*, then the 1970s flop *Lovely Ladies, Kind Gentlemen*, based on a book called *The Teahouse of the August Moon*; it centred round a government funded programme to Americanize the Japanese after World War Two, but its racial stereotypes proved intolerable to audiences thirty years later.

Flush from their success with *Funny Girl*, composer Jule Styne and lyricist Bob Merrill wrote a musical version of *Some Like It Hot*, retitled *Sugar*, which flopped in '72, possibly because the film version was so definitive there really was nothing to add to it. In '74 the Jerry Herman/Michael Stewart musical *Mack and Mabel* nosedived, despite containing hit songs such as 'Movies Were Movies' and 'Tap Your Troubles Away'. But it was an inferior version of *A Chorus Line* and too out of step with the glam rock era; by '74 new musicals were looking badly outdated. Not even Liza Minnelli and Barry Nelson got anywhere in a musical called *The Act*, the story of a Vegas cabaret artist written by Kander and Ebb and directed by Martin Scorsese; Minnelli won a Tony for her role, but audiences weren't interested.

In '78 the musical *Ballroom*, by Alan and Marilyn Bergman and based on a TV movie set in an old-fashioned dance club in the Bronx, was so dreadful it picked up an immediate cult following. But the critics and the majority of theatregoers thought it too whimsical and stayed away. Then came Richard Rodgers's last show, *I Remember Mama*, a nostalgic musical about a family in turn of the century San Francisco; a disastrous revival of *Brigadoon*; seven years of *42nd Street* – and then Lloyd Webber moved into the Majestic with *The Phantom of the Opera*.

Bad/good

What one generally means by bad/good musicals is the juggernaut, the hugely expensive, hugely lucrative super-musical that takes the same approach to theatre as McDonald's does to catering: they are available in identical format, in every big tourist centre in the world, endlessly franchised and reproduced, despite sneering from the critics. Lloyd Webber, in other words.

I have mixed feelings about Lloyd Webber.

In January 2006 *The Phantom of the Opera* broke the record for the longest-running show in Broadway history, overtaking *Cats* and reminding us what real entertainment is about: candles, dry ice, big hair and the sort of synthesized chord progressions only achieved by a collapse at the keyboard. The original novel, by Gaston Leroux, is set in nineteenth-century Paris, but the Lloyd Webber adaptation harks unmistakably back to 1986. It was Lloyd Webber's sixth major musical and his last real blockbuster. (The lyrics are by Charles Hart – Lloyd Webber and Tim Rice split ten years earlier, after *Evita*.)

Of all his stage shows, it is the one that strives most greedily for the status of a higher art form and this explains its success, too; for what it is, *Phantom* feels quite posh and its pretensions flatter its audience without making them feel uncomfortable. In the title song the phantom is shown to be flesh and blood and also 'there, inside your mind'. He is a man and at the same time a metaphor; he is the 'Angel of Music', but he looks like the devil. Make of this what you will. Personally I think it's about the importance of not judging people by appearances, although the moral is undermined somewhat when the phantom goes on a killing spree after being turned down for a date by Christine.

My fondness for the show is influenced by my nostalgia for the first time I saw it, as a child, when Michael Crawford was the lead. I like the score to *Phantom* and I like the show. It is Lloyd Webber's best, I think, because there are more than two good tunes and the story is fantastical enough to suit, rather than grate against, its composer's occasionally histrionic style. (Quiet bit, quiet bit, quiet bit, SUDDEN VERY LOUD BIT, MASSIVE CLIMAX, quiet bit, quiet bit, fade to end.) My favourite bit is the auction at the beginning, before the chandelier crashes down, when the auctioneer says, 'Lot 665, ladies and gentlemen, a papier mâché music box in the shape of a barrel organ,' and the monkey on it plays a wistful little tune and the effect is genuinely sinister. In 2004, *The Phantom of the Opera* was made into a film, directed by Joel Schumacher and starring Gerard Butler and

Emmy Rossum. I found it on a cable TV station in a hotel in San Francisco and settled down happily to relive the magic while I cleared out the snacks from the minibar.

God, it was terrible; like an extended pop video for '80s rock band Heart. The phantom looked like Worzel Gummidge, Christine looked like Jennifer Rush and the main chorus girl, Meg, was Jennifer Ellison off *Brookside*, who kept asking the leading lady, 'Who is your great chewtor?' (Of course she'd been chewtored secretly all this while by the phantom.) Nobody sang, they shouted, as if they were still in a theatre and had to project to the cheap seats. I was rooting for the phantom over the wimpish Raoul, that is until his mask came off and, as he cringed and cowered, the camera zoomed in. His horrific scar was no worse than a blister aggravated by what looked like bad sunburn. I suppose the makers of the film calculated that anything more gruesome would jeopardize its family rating. But the whole thing fell apart then and kept nosediving until the scene in which Christine sees herself dressed as a bride and keels over, Raoul tells her this man, this thing, is not your father, they fall through a trap door into a pool of water, where the poor old phantom chases her around a bit and Christine kisses him, bringing on his long overdue breakdown. He realizes that she can only pity, not love him, then he goes mental at her and next thing you know they're in a graveyard with snow, rose petals, a stallion, some candles and a reprise of the title song. It looks a bit like a Flake advert.

The only super-musical to have come close to the success of Lloyd Webber is *Les Misérables*. It too is based on upmarket source material, the mid-nineteenth-century book of the same name by Victor Hugo, and was turned into a stage musical in 1980 with music by Claude-Michel Schonberg and lyrics by Alain Boublil. The pair also wrote *Miss Saigon* and the less successful *Martin Guerre*.

Like *Phantom*, *Les Mis* doesn't stint on production values, so that the portentousness of the lyrics and the melodrama of the action are matched by grandiosity in every other aspect of the show. Super-musicals understand that if a character is going to stand centre stage and promise a disaster 'beyond your imagination', then he damn well better deliver it. But whereas the story in *Phantom* is fantastical, *Les Mis* strives towards realism. 'Desperation is bounded only by the flimsiest of walls . . .' wrote Victor Hugo. 'They appear utterly depraved, vile and odious; it is rare for those who have sunk so low not to be degraded in the process and there comes a point, moreover, where the unfortunate and infamous are grouped together, merged in a single fateful world. They are the outcasts, the underdogs, les Misérables.'

Les Mis is generally considered to be a cut above Lloyd Webber because it is based on real historical events, which it tries to make some serious points about. Those points don't seem to have registered, since even people who have seen it three times still labour under the delusion that it's about the French Revolution. (It is set just after the July Revolution, thirty years later.) I first saw *Les Mis* on a school trip in 1990, when the sight of all those people gasping one last tune on the barricades was even more embarrassing than the production of *A Midsummer Night's Dream* we'd gone to in which all the actors were naked. Where other modern shows get by on two good songs, *Les Mis* churns them out one after the other: the score is really very good. But it is also very, very long, like reliving the revolution in real time: along with a massacre you get two ghosts, a suicide, a child shot in the leg and made to drag himself across the stage, three further death scenes, each more aerobic than the last and always prefaced by a sort of black power salute and a hammy collapse into oblivion, singing prostitutes, jolly poor people, a chase between Valjean and the policeman Javert, the rousing anthem 'One Day More' and the pitiful exit of Fantine. 'Look, monsieur, where all the children play!' she raves in her white nightie and her eyes roll heavenwards.

I went to see it again after a fifteen-year interlude. Since its first performance at the Barbican, the show has made over £1bn in thirty-eight countries and I can see more clearly now why. Apart from the catchiness of the tunes, its success has to do with the adaptability of its sentiments, the ease with which a modern audience might watch it and say, this is actually about me. A man imprisoned for stealing bread, woefully hard done by, who overcomes his circumstances to become mayor and yet, despite his respectability, sides with the Parisian rioters – it's the definition of the bourgeois bohemian, wealthy but noble, always on the side of the underdog but with a nice house, too. Jean Valjean has his cake and eats it and the musical makes it easy for the audience to feel smug about themselves; the principle of justice would be more powerfully made if Valjean had been imprisoned for stealing candlesticks to fund his heroin habit, rather than to feed his dying family.

There is still a problem with the barricade scenes, mainly because there is no historical context; the date is flashed up on the wall, but nothing else. When the noble students rise up in defence of the poor it plays like a one-size-fits-all piece of motivational life coaching, with the 'barricades' offered as a metaphor for whatever might be troubling you at the time. I found all the starving/singing people as embarrassing the second time round as I had the first. It reminded me of a GCSE drama class in which we had to pretend to be *sans-culottes*, running around in our school uniforms screaming 'Bread! bread!' before breaking for lunch.

I expected the Queen's Theatre to be half empty. Are there really enough people in the world who want to see *Les Mis* a fourth time? But it was almost full. And although competition for able singers is intense in London, with seventeen other musicals hoovering up the talent, the current cast of *Les Mis* has at least three strong voices and only one shrieker. There was a standing ovation at the end.

The most interesting thing about *Les Mis* is that the real love story is not between Marius and Cosette but between Valjean and Javert, the policeman who hounds him across France. Some kind of inverse Stockholm syndrome takes hold of Javert, whose hatred of Valjean is so bright and undiminishing that when Valjean ends their relationship by sparing Javert's life, the policeman is destroyed. The duet they sing at this point is a twisted kind of love song after which Javert commits suicide. The world he has known is lost in shadow, he says and dives into the river.

Phantom and *Les Mis* were the progenitors of a look now mandatory for expensive stage musicals: one dominated by huge, moving sets and a revolving stage. Another super-musical to follow in their footsteps is *Wicked*, a prequel to *The Wizard of Oz*, which does for the witch of the west what *Wide Sargasso Sea* did for Bertha Mason. It is in its third year and looks likely to go on and on.

Good/bad

A lot of people who've seen it consider Neil Diamond's 1980 remake of *The Jazz Singer* to be one of the worst films ever made, and it's certainly right up there with *Brigadoon*. Richard Fleischer, the director, had previous form for the biopic *Che!*, in which the South American revolutionary was played by Omar Sharif and Fidel Castro by (wait for it) Jack Palance. But in *The Jazz Singer*, he rose to a whole new level of miscasting, with Neil Diamond as a trainee synagogue cantor who wants to be a rock star, to the horror of his orthodox Jewish father played with more than a nod to Shylock by Laurence Olivier.

So you see, there were problems.

How you feel about *The Jazz Singer* is largely going to depend on how you feel about Neil Diamond. Before I saw the film, I was non-committal. I didn't really know who he was beyond the fact that he duetted with Streisand in 'You Don't Bring Me Flowers', and often mixed him up with Neil Sedaka. I didn't know that he had this legendary status as bad taste personified, although it wasn't long into the film before I started catching on. It's hard to figure out what it is that distinguishes the so-bad-it's-good category from the just plain awful. Why is *The Jazz Singer* great, but the film version of *Phantom* terrible? I think it's something to do with good faith; what saves *The*

Jazz Singer from awfulness is its combination of 100 per cent self-belief with 0 per cent self-awareness. Whereas Neil Diamond really believes in what he's doing, the actors in the film of *Phantom* seem to know they've got a turkey on their hands; they believe in themselves all right, as all good graduates of stage school do, but they don't believe in their material. Neil Diamond appears to believe in everything, bless him. And you can't help loving it.

So it is that, in the opening scenes, we are introduced to Jesse Rabinovitch, a young man in an orthodox Jewish neighbourhood in New York, who is struggling to assert himself against the authority of his father. (Jesse's mother was killed in a 'playground massacre' which is never explained.) He feels that his life, which revolves around the synagogue and his conventional wife, is suffocating him. Although at the time of making the film Diamond is almost forty, he complains that he has lost 'the groove'.

Enter Laurence Olivier, stage left, in carpet slippers and milk bottle glasses. To establish his whimsical Yiddish nature and also his grasp of the accent, he says things like, 'Harry Truman vhas a vhunderful man.' He blinks rapidly. He tells his rebellious son, who wants to anglicize his name to Jess Robin, 'If you don't know vhere you've come from, how do you know vhere you are going?' Jesse's only outlet is the band he plays in, a soul group in which he is the single white member. When he plays gigs with the group in Harlem he disguises himself as a black man with boot polish and a rasta wig. Someone in the crowd senses that the third guy to the left doesn't have all the moves and yells, 'He ain't no brother – he's a white boy!' and chases him down the street. You really never know what's going to happen next in *The Jazz Singer*.

Jesse flies to LA to try to get a record deal. It's in the film's favour that, unlike so many easy listening stars who try to pull off 'rock' musicals, Diamond had the good sense not to position himself too far from his actual fan base. When Jesse gets the chance to perform in front of a big audience, the production doesn't lose its head and put him in a stadium. Instead, it has him perform in a nice, comfy, indoor arena, where the audience is seated and claps politely after each number. Compare this to, for example, Bette Midler's grotesque attempt to play Janis Joplin in *The Rose* (Alan Bates plays her manager), in which she ranges around the place snarling 'fuck this shit' while all you can think is, this is a woman whose first LP was produced by Barry Manilow. Likewise, although it pains me to say it, Streisand's misconceived role as a 'rocker' in the *A Star is Born* remake, in which she, too, has a stab at swearing and singing rock anthems. It's like casting Michael Ball in a biopic of Mick Jagger.

Neil Diamond doesn't try to be hip. While in LA, he gets a female manager who shares his vision for 1970s soft rock and whom he considers ditching his square wife for. She gets him some gigs and in good, solid musicals tradition Diamond wins round a hostile crowd with his ballad 'Summer Love'. He says, 'I can't go back now,' and grins. 'Just look at him!' says his square wife, Rivka, who flies to LA to try to win him back and sure enough, there he is, in his purple metallic shirt with the puffed sleeves, singing to the gently swaying, seated audience. Then he sings 'Love on the Rocks', which really isn't a bad record.

Eventually, Jesse ditches his wife and moves in with Molly the female manager. This provokes Laurence Olivier to fly out to LA in his carpet slippers. He bursts into his son's beachside condo, heads straight for the piano and hammers out a religious tune. Jesse says he won't return to New York with Olivier, who then tears off a square of his shirt and tells his son he is dead to him. He storms out. Molly says, 'Who's dead?'

'I am,' replies Diamond, looking hurt and pensive, and he runs away to have a booze-fuelled breakdown, playing in third rate bars where his lounge act gets booed and his taste in shirts mocked by rednecks. Eventually news reaches him that, in another fine tradition of the musical, Molly has given birth to a son, his son, and he must pull himself together now and be a man. He returns to the beachside condo and assumes his responsibilities as a father.

In the final scene of *The Jazz Singer*, Diamond gets booked for a gig and one final shot at the big time. What with the arrival of his first grandchild, Laurence Olivier is persuaded to bury the hatchet and fly out for the concert. Diamond stands on stage in a blue sequined shirt, hand on hip, while the audience sways like a metronome and Olivier, skull cap pushed far back on his head, strokes his chin not quite in time. He's supposed to be thinking, so; this is vhat the young people are listening to today . . . it's not bad, not bad at all. What he's actually thinking, of course, while Diamond croons 'Coming To America', is that he once played Othello to Maggie Smith's Desdemona. He is reliving the ovation he enjoyed at the Old Vic after the battle scene in *Henry V*. He is doing everything he can just to keep himself from crying.

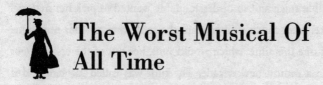

The Worst Musical Of All Time

What Would Barbra Do?

enerally speaking, bad film musicals are never quite as bad as bad stage productions; there is something about actors performing to an empty theatre or to a sniggering live audience that film flops can't touch for cruelty. At least, most of them can't. There is one film musical, however, which the experience of watching on TV is every bit as painful to endure as the worst stage flop: *Xanadu*.

In 1980, two years after the release of *Grease*, Olivia Newton-John was still searching for the perfect follow-up film. She was Hollywood gold at that stage and so understandably wanted to pick her material with care. After much deliberation, she settled on another musical, a modern one this time, which would yank her out of the ersatz 1950s and into a radical new decade. The film was called *Xanadu* and it would advertise its modernity by taking place mostly on roller skates. Gene Kelly, at seventy, was somehow persuaded to sign up and the male lead was given to an unknown TV actor called Michael Beck. It was directed by Robert Greenwald, who had made three TV movies at that stage, among them *Sharon: Portrait of a Mistress* and *Katie: Portrait of a Centrefold*. *Xanadu* was promoted as 'a fantasy, a musical, a place where dreams come true' and featured a soundtrack by the Electric Light Orchestra, Cliff Richard and a band called the Tubes. It tried so hard to be cool that you could almost see the vein standing out on its head.

It is set in Santa Monica, where a commercial artist called Sonny Malone (Michael Beck) dreams of being the next Michelangelo, but is frustrated by the philistine demands of his day job. His boss is always yelling at him to 'meet the deadline', but Sonny's attitude is c'mon man, art has no deadline. He takes a sabbatical to work on his masterpiece, but all he comes up with is a really bad line drawing of a woman with big hair, which he tears up in disgust. Strange things happen to torn up paper in musicals and the wind carries his sketch into the sky to return in human form; specifically, as Olivia Newton-John, on roller skates.

Just like in the picture her hair is a static-crazed mushroom cloud and Sonny keeps seeing her through the crowds. Who *is* that mysterious woman? Then while walking on the beach one day, Sonny bumps into an old guy in a nasty cardigan playing the clarinet on a rock, just jamming along by himself with an air of sadness and regret. Poor Gene Kelly. How they persuaded him to take part is a mystery, but his expression at every stage of the film is one of utter bewilderment. Sonny and Gene get chatting and the old guy suggests that sometimes the best person to tell your troubles to is a stranger. 'C'mon, what's on your mind?'

Sonny tells him about his frustrations as an artist. Gene says, 'Hey, do you like Glenn Miller?' Sonny replies, 'Do you like rock 'n' roll?' and they smile at each other in acknowledgement of the generation gap and the possibility that, who knows, maybe it's not as big as everyone makes out.

Gene, it transpires, was once a successful musician with the Tommy Dorsey band and Glenn Miller himself, but abandoned his dream in order to 'go into industry', which the film presents as a sort of nervous breakdown, where he made lots of money but was

Unfulfilled. He has flashbacks to the big band era and then the plot does a massive lurch and Gene announces he's going to open a club in LA and asks Sonny to be his partner. Sonny resigns from his commercial art job ('Shit,' says his boss, hurling down a paint brush, because Sonny was good, real good, maybe one of the best) and throws in his lot with Gene and still Olivia Newton-John keeps appearing at odd intervals, dressed in an off-the-shoulder peasant shirt and travelling at speed. Who knew it was possible to roller-skate enigmatically? Sonny eventually manages to catch up with her and they roller-skate through town together, singing 'Suddenly the Wheels are in Motion' ('and I'm ready to sail any ocean').

Gene's vision of the club is as an upscale big-band dance hall. But Sonny says: 'No! A rock 'n' roll band. This is the '80s!' And so the two music styles go head to head in a fantasy number in which a Cyd Charisse type figure from the '40s takes part in a dance-off with '80s go-go dancers and what you realize, suddenly, is how amazingly similar they are, matching each other for raunch and dexterity. And it's all part of the wonderful continuum that is American pop culture.

But what to call the new club? Gene wanders around the derelict venue trying to come up with a name. All of a sudden, Olivia Newton-John appears and says robotically, as if channelling a higher spirit, 'In Xanadu did Kubla Khan a stately pleasure-dome decree.' And Gene, who's up on his Coleridge too, continues in a sort of reverie, 'Where Alph the sacred river ran through caverns measureless to man down to a sunless sea.' Of course! The place should be called Xanadu!

Construction starts and even the builders have picked up on the metaphorical undercurrents of this baby, as the foreman turns to Gene and says, 'You know, when you guys told me you were building a dream, I thought you were crazy.' Gene says he'd like to dance on opening night and Sonny says, with a wink at the audience, 'You? Dance?' and Gene says something like, I've been known to tap my toes now and then. God, they really rub his nose in it. But of course the film isn't really interested in him, so he is given a quick number in which, in a tragic reprise of *An American in Paris*, he gets to roller-skate in circles to the Electric Light Orchestra, looking creaky and demoralized but carrying gamely on. And then Newton-John shoves him aside for her big number.

At this point she thinks it's time to get honest with Sonny. With a faraway look in her eye she explains that she comes from 'Mount Helicon' and is the 'daughter of Zeus'. So *that's* why she has never invited him to her apartment. Sonny stares at her and the writers suffer a small crisis of faith in their audience. When Newton-John tells Sonny she is his muse, she suggests that he 'look up "muse" in the dictionary', which he does and reads out the definition. Like the Little Mermaid, it turns out that Olivia Newton-John can't survive on earth and has to go back to where she came from; back to heaven. And guess what heaven looks like? A 1980s roller disco.

Sonny is dejected. 'Dreams die,' he says. But Gene, drawing on his experience of the golden age, yells, 'No. No. Not by themselves. We kill them.' And then he says: 'Kid, it's up to you.'

Sonny has to get to heaven, he just has to, and as luck would have it, he's skating through Santa Monica one day and sees a wall decorated by graffiti artists with a picture of the eight muses. He goes out on a limb and takes this to be a portal of some kind. Sonny skates smack into the wall and suddenly he's in the roller disco of destiny, all dark but for orange neon strip lighting. 'Hey, Zeus!' he calls. 'Zeus! I've come to get Kira.' And Olivia Newton-John tells him, you don't understand, I can't come with you. They sing a song about doomed love. Then Zeus's wife tells him to let the kids do what they want and so they beam back down to the club where the finale takes place, an attempt at a Busby Berkeley type number, only with strobe lighting and lots of extras in leg-warmers. Gene Kelly is in a tux, roller-skating for all he's worth, but the look on his face is blind panic. Olivia Newton-John sings about a dream that has grown over a million 'years', and has survived all their 'tears'. And it ends with Sonny sitting in a booth and Olivia Newton-John appearing as his waitress, the implication being that she is mortal now and has to earn a living and they smile at each other as if to say: to the future!

The Aquamusical

What Would Barbra Do?

The sub-category of Hollywood blockbuster known as the 'aquamusical' had a short but vivid life. If you have ever seen one, it won't surprise you to learn that at the height of its popularity in the '40s and '50s there was widespread LSD abuse going on in Hollywood. The marriage of water-based stunts – aqua-batics – with all the regular charms of the musical gripped the box office like nothing else in the post-war period. Aquamusicals grew out of the success of Billy Rose's aquacade, the huge tank he introduced to audiences at the 1939 New York World's Fair, in which aquabelles and aquabeaux dived and swam in complex routines. Other novelty musicals had been tried in the past – the Norwegian Olympic skating champion Sonja Henie made some ice-based musicals including *Happy Landing* and *Thin Ice*, in which she played opposite Tyrone Power. But it was the aquamusicals that really caught the imagination of the post-war audience and, forty years later, me.

The most famous of Billy Rose's aquabelles was Esther Williams and the most famous aquabeau Johnny Weissmuller, who would go on to find fame in the TV series *Tarzan*. I forgot about Williams the moment I grew too vain about my hair to keep swimming competitively. And then, quite recently, I was in a second-hand bookshop in north London and stumbled across a book called *The Million Dollar Mermaid*, with a familiar gold-clad figure on the cover. I bought it for old times' sake, imagining it would be too terrible to read. But two pages in and I was lost for the afternoon. I have not read a book that has given me such pleasure for a very long time.

Williams, it turns out, was every bit as worthwhile a heroine as I had reckoned her, on the basis of her swimming hats, to be. Like all great heroines, her back-story was in real life much more dramatic than anything the scriptwriters came up with for her. Her mother was a formidable woman, born Bula Myrtle Gilpin, the ninth of twelve children, and her father, Louis, came from a poor farming family. After marrying, they moved from Kansas to Los Angeles with their five children, including Williams's brother Stanton, who was starting to get work as a child actor. But he died, and with him a big slice of the family income. There were four other children, including a sister whom Williams, the youngest, described rather arrestingly in the book as a 'malcontent'. When she was thirteen, Williams was raped by a sixteen-year-old lodger they rented her late brother's old room to. She channelled her disgust and fury into competitive swimming at the LA Athletic Club. I read on, enthralled. By the time she was eighteen Williams was a champion speed swimmer in the 100 metre freestyle and 400 metre relay events. She was due to compete at the 1940 Olympic Games but then World War Two broke out, and the Olympics were cancelled. She had a job lined up in a department store when Billy Rose rang. He was recruiting for his aquacade and, having asked around for pretty swimming champions, invited her to audition. Her swimming was superlative but Rose didn't like her stocky physique. 'Sir,' she told him, smartly, 'if you're not strong enough to swim fast then you're probably not strong enough to swim pretty.'

The aquacade wasn't the heaven on earth that I had imagined it to be, but a nightmare of draughty dressing rooms, dangerous dives and the almost constant sexual harassment of the aquabelles by the aquabeaux. Unbelievable! Williams's memoir is a masterpiece of a particular kind of brittle, Hollywood humour that people who are required to expose themselves for a living assume as a defensive cloak. She comes across as a sort of Bette Davis of the high diving board. The book is full of lines like, 'I should have known my next picture would be trouble as soon as the Mexican tailor demanded that my bosom would have to go,' and, 'Nobody ever thought of anyone as gay back then, we just thought of Sydney as, well, grand.'

When Howard Hughes tried to back her into a corner and seduce her, she blew him off with a casual, 'Don't even try, Howard, I'm too athletic.'

After success with Billy Rose's show, she was picked up by Hollywood and films such as *Skirts Ahoy!* and *Neptune's Daughter* turned Williams into one of the biggest box office stars of the early 1950s. Her biggest hit of all was *Million Dollar Mermaid*, in which she played real-life Australian swimming champion Annette Kellerman. Kellerman, a forerunner to Williams, had introduced herself to London audiences by ploughing seventeen miles up the Thames. She made three attempts at swimming the Channel before going to Hollywood and making it as the swimming star of silent movies such as *Siren of the Sea*. At the height of her popularity she was arrested on Boston beach for indecency and the ensuing outcry ushered in a new era in progressive attitudes towards women's swimwear.

It turns out that the scene I had tried to replicate on the high-diving board at my local pool had nearly killed Williams when she shot it during *Million Dollar Mermaid*. In the famous trapeze scene so dear to my heart, the gold-painted crown she wore was made out of tin, not cardboard. It was only when she was fifty feet up and swinging from the trapeze that Williams realized the implications of this: when she hit the water, it was likely the tin would stay rigid and the shock of impact would be absorbed wholly by her neck. But Busby Berkeley was shouting at her through a megaphone to dive, goddamnit, dive, and although she couldn't see the tank through the plumes of coloured smoke, she dived, blind, hoping she wouldn't miss the small pool and smash straight into concrete. The effect of the tin crown on her head was much the same as if she had. As anticipated, the impact of the heavy crown's hitting the water travelled down her neck and snapped three vertebrae. She was in a body cast for six months, after which she emerged, in what must be the epitome of show-must-go-on bravado, to finish the picture.

I put down the book and swallowed hard a few times.

It also turns out that it wasn't, actually, Williams in that seminal scene at the end of *Easy to Love*. At the time of filming in Florida she was five months pregnant and put her foot down when Berkeley once more tried to get her to risk her life in a crazy high-dive. She had nearly had her face shaved off during the waterskiing scene, when the propellers of the camera boat got too near to her skis. Just under the surface were needle-sharp geysers shooting jets of water into the air, which threatened, if she fell, to impale her. She told Berkeley to get a stunt double.

'I hate stunt doubles,' he grumbled, to which Williams replied, 'Not as much as I hate miscarriages.'

What Would Barbra Do?

The scene was played, instead, by a champion platform diver called Helen Crelinkovich, who had to be paid three thousand dollars each time she dived from the trapeze that was attached to the passing helicopter that lifted her one hundred feet in the air. She did it in three takes.

'I would have preferred stronger leading men,' wrote Williams, in summary of her career, 'but it's quite possible that a more prominent actor wouldn't want to hold my towel.' Her favourite leading man was, she said, 'the water'. In later years she would try to make it without much success as a dramatic actress in films such as *Raw Wind in Eden* and devoted her retirement years to campaigning to get synchronized swimming recognized as an Olympic event. She is in her eighties now and still lives in Los Angeles. I have an image of her, diving through the smoke like an arrow, not knowing if there is water on the other side or cement. When I was nine it struck me as the apex of all human achievement and it still, to some extent, does.

Lili

What Would Barbra Do?

There was a song my mother sang that stood out in her repertoire purely because she knew all the words to it. She said it was from a musical, but beyond the fact that it starred Leslie Caron, she was sketchy about the details or even the title of the film and since it never, in all my years living at home, showed up on TV, I assumed it was some barmy thing from an era more bygone than usual.

For some reason it had stuck, however, and on light summer evenings she would fold sheets and sing this song called 'Hi Lili, Hi Lo' about a girl sitting by the window and watching the rain and musing about how she would probably never love again.

My mother moved her head from side to side. 'Don't you like it?'

'Hmm,' I said.

Then last year a friend of mine listed among her favourite musicals one called *Lili*. 'Starring Leslie Caron,' she said. She had it on video.

It is barely ninety minutes long and based on a story by Paul Gallico. The plot is paper-thin. The dialogue is short and epigrammatic, so that it all seems rather dreamlike. Leslie Caron is an orphaned sixteen-year-old who blows into a French provincial town with a scrap of paper on which is written the name and address of a friend of her late father's. He runs a bakery and she hopes he will take her in. But when she arrives at his door she finds out, to her horror, that he has recently died and she is invited in to recover by the kindly proprietor of the shop next door. 'I'm very strong,' she pleads. 'I'm a hard worker. I can work very hard without getting a bit tired!'

The kindly proprietor gives her a plate of lunch. He tells her she can earn her keep in the shop, only while explaining this he moves a little closer and one suddenly notices how fat he is, how red in the face and how his eyes bulge. Soon he is chasing Lili round the cash register and she is only saved by a customer who has come in to buy a handkerchief. As she follows her rescuer outside, the proprietor swears at her retreating back. Seeing how upset she is, the rescuer makes his handkerchief appear out of her ear. She smiles, uncertainly.

'It is a trick?'

He nods and makes a little bow. 'Farewell, mademoiselle,' he says. 'You are young! It's a fine day. And tomorrow will be another.'

Lili watches as he and his two friends walk down the street. She doesn't share his optimism. After all, it is easy for him to say. She starts to follow them and the magician's friends tease him until eventually he turns round and tells her to run along home. Lili explains she is an orphan and has nowhere to go and eventually they allow her to come with them, to the travelling carnival where they work and where she gets a job as a waitress.

The carnival is a seedy place, full of people who dreamed of going into show business a little higher up the ladder than this. They are hard and garish, like carnival colours. Lili's saviour works there under the stage-name Marco the Magnificent, assisted on stage by Zsa Zsa Gabor. Lili is so busy staring at Marco during his performance that she is fired for bad waitressing. She walks out of the tent, picks up her suitcase and, with nowhere to go and no one to turn to, starts slowly to climb a ladder with the intention of throwing herself from the top.

What Would Barbra Do?

It is at this stage that something strange happens. A voice calls to her and, looking down, she sees a small man with red hair, not two feet high, signalling for her to come over. He is on the stage of a puppet theatre. Momentarily distracted, she goes over to the man and he starts to talk to her, calling over his friends: a fox, an ogre and a small woman called Marguerite, who warns her that the fox is not to be trusted because he is a 'seducer'. Slowly, Lili becomes entranced. The puppets work to cheer her up and ask if she knows any songs. She says she does not. 'You must know a song,' says Carrot Top, the chief puppet. She thinks and eventually says, 'It's just an old song. I used to sing it with my father. Hi lili, hi lo.' And she sings it to the puppets.

It is such a sweet song, sung by Lili in her straw hat and poor clothes, that unbeknownst to her a crowd of off-duty performers starts gathering behind her, transfixed. The melody is like a lullaby and contrasts painfully with the words, which speak of only adult disappointments. As she sings in a small, sad voice the crowd swells. At the end of the song, they applaud and Lili looks round, astonished. Inside the puppet theatre, behind the curtain, the man manipulating the puppets wears a stunned expression. He nods at his puppets helplessly, as if to say, yes, it's love.

Lili is incorporated into the puppet show and every afternoon affects to wander past and be, as if by chance, incorporated into the action. She always ends by singing the song. The audiences grow and grow, as word of this small act spreads and people find it more bewitching than the sophisticated thrills of the carnival.

Meanwhile all Lili dreams of is Marco the Magnificent. He toys with her, flirting when it suits him then retreating to his trailer with Zsa Zsa Gabor. Paul Berthalet the puppet-master sees all this and is furious. He is lame in one leg from a war injury, which ended his career as France's most famous male ballet star and turned him into a bitter alcoholic with a low-rent carnival act. 'Disenchanted, disappointed, but going on like a dog chasing a stick!' he cries one day in his trailer, lashing out at Lili, who refers to him as 'the angry man'. Berthalet's friend Jacquot tells him, 'You're in love with the girl and she's in love with someone else. It happens all the time. People don't die of love.' But Berthalet is being eaten alive watching Lili strive after the unworthy magician. One day during the show, he asks Lili, through one of the puppets, what she most wants in the world. She says she doesn't know. He presses her. Still she says she doesn't know. 'I think,' says the puppet quietly, 'you'd like one day to have the feeling of being loved. That someone cared what happened to you.' The audience is very still. Lili looks upset. Then a child in the audience pipes up, 'I care!' And a woman says, 'I care.' And a fusty old bloke clears his throat and in spite of himself says, 'I care.'

In the audience that day is the biggest theatrical impresario in France. So impressed is he by the act that he approaches Berthalet backstage. He asks about Lili and Jacquot explains that 'she's like a little bell that gives off a pure sound. She lives each show.' The producers offer the two men a fortune to come to Paris to perform at the nation's most prestigious venue: the Folies Bergères. Paul Berthalet is moved almost to tears. 'Say it again . . .' he whispers to his benefactors.

'You mean,' says a benefactor, 'that you've chosen a new career that will outstrip anything you've done as a dancer?'

He shakes his head in amazement. 'And you said that before you knew I was lame.'

Without the girl, however, the act is nothing and while all this has been going on Lili has decided to leave, after another titanic fight with Berthalet. For it transpires that the magician and Zsa Zsa Gabor were actually married all this while. When Lili found out she was broken-hearted, which sent Paul Berthalet into such a jealous rage that he slapped her.

'What do you know about love?' she screamed and now, Jacquot tells Berthalet, she is packing. Berthalet panics – he needs her for his show, but more than that, he needs her for his life, for his love. As Lili passes the puppet theatre carrying her little suitcase, Berthalet dives behind the curtain as he did the day of her suicidal urge. He calls to her. Reluctantly, she comes over. As Carrot Top the puppet he says, 'It was love at first sight. When I saw you wearing that . . . awful hat.'

'You're the only things I love,' she says, hugging the puppets, and then comes to her senses and pulling down the curtain says furiously to Paul Berthalet, 'I must be crazy. But they're so very dear to me . . . I forget.' She screams at him as if he has deceived her. 'Why do you hide behind the puppets?'

He screams back, 'I *am* the puppets,' rather as Cathy screams, 'Nelly, I *am* Heathcliff.' Because all this time Berthalet has been using the puppets to speak his true feelings without fear of rejection or ridicule.

Lili

Lili runs away, out of the carnival and onto the road where she keeps on running and while running she has a dream in which she has to choose between Paul Berthalet and the magician. And she realizes while dreaming that the one she wants is Berthalet, that he is real and the magician is false. Echoing the bible, prefiguring the Byrds, she says, 'There's a time for going to school, for losing our parents, for falling in love with a beautiful magician. And there is a time for waking up.

'We don't learn,' says Lili. 'We just get older. Then we know.'

And so she runs back to the carnival and jumps into Paul Berthalet's arms and they kiss and that's the end, except that while they're kissing, the puppets stand up in the theatre and clap without anyone working them, as if, like Tinkerbell in *Peter Pan*, the fact of believing in them was sufficient to make them real.

The Sound of Music

The Sound of Music

Pretoria State Theatre is in the centre of South Africa's capital, a big, chaotic town carved up by arterial roads and overlooked from a hill by the parliament building. One afternoon, while on holiday there, I went to the State Theatre with my aunt and two friends of hers, to see a matinee performance of *The Sound of Music*. The captain was to be played by a South African pop star and Neil Diamond impersonator called Steve Hofmeyr, who was billed in the programme as a 'controversial singer, actor, songwriter, presenter, poet, writer, polemicist, activist, issue-ist and father'. When I mentioned his name to South Africans my age, they clutched their sides and fell about with laughter.

I had never seen a live performance of *The Sound of Music* before – it is difficult to stage, what with the logistical problems and the unshakeable images everyone has in their heads of the film. The only way I could imagine it working was if it was so radically different from the Julie Andrews version that it brought new meaning to the story. But I couldn't imagine what this might be.

From his photo, I gathered that Hofmeyr was South Africa's answer to David Hasselhoff. According to the programme he had a big following in Belgium, where his duet with local singer Dana Winter charted at number two. His philosophy was 'Ek lewe my gat af, en jy', which one of my aunt's friends translated for me, rather perplexingly, as 'I live my arse off, and you?' Just before the show started, Sharon, my aunt's other friend, got up to go to the loo. 'Leave your bag,' said my aunt.

'I can't.' Sharon sniffed. 'It's got a gun in it.'

She came back and the overture began and we sat there, in the front row, armed and ready, while I wondered why it was that my experience of *The Sound of Music* was always linked to the possible outbreak of violence.

The actress playing Maria went for the English accent. The nuns spoke in broad Afrikaans. Steve Hofmeyr waxed Germanic and Uncle Max seemed to be basing his performance on Topol in *Fiddler on the Roof*. With his moustache and squat figure he looked like a member of the security police.

The first half of the show was faithful to the film and not bad, really, save for a bit of feedback on the mikes. The voices were strong, especially among the nuns who had been borrowed from the opera house. When the von Trapp children ran across the stage, the theatre shook. There is capacity for over one thousand people in the auditorium and it was full, that day. This was the theatre's biggest production of the year and there was a lot of buzz around it. We milled about in the foyer at the interval as children ran about in fancy dress – many of their mothers had put them in lederhosen for the occasion and they were over-excited and screamy. Sharon clutched her bag to her chest.

The second half started with the scene on the terrace of the von Trapp villa, when Maria returns from the abbey resolved to address her feelings for the captain. I didn't notice the change at first; it was too subtle. A ripple ran across the surface of the audience and the odd hair shot up on the back of the odd neck. Slowly, incrementally, something began to happen. Steve Hofmeyr's German accent began discreetly to soften. His body language relaxed. Before our eyes, the man began to change.

The emotional climax of the film is the scene at the music festival when the captain stands on stage and breaks down during 'Edelweiss'. The show looked as if it was going to stay faithful to this. Two swastikas unfurled at the back of the stage and Hofmeyr stood in the centre, alone, his feet widely planted. He began to sing 'Edelweiss'. By now his accent was full-blown American and he keened slightly, moved by the power of his own performance. As he crooned his way into the second verse with a long sustain on the word 'fore-e-e-e-ver' it became suddenly clear what was happening: he was doing the captain *as Neil Diamond*.

The afternoon shot instantly into the top five best of my life.

The thing one forgets about Maria Augusta Kutschera, married name von Trapp, is that she was really a very religious woman indeed. Not religious in the scatty, offhand way that Julie Andrews played her. Religious in a heavy, Bavarian way that made it hard to imagine her singing 'Do-Re-Mi' or choosing, as a preferred method of movement, skipping. It is a little known fact that, as well as writing the memoir on which *The Sound of Music* was based, Maria von Trapp wrote several other books, including *Yesterday, Today and Forever: The Religious Life of a Remarkable Family*, *Let Me Tell You About My Saviour*, and *When the King Was Carpenter*, a study of the life of Christ.

It was in 1949 that the memoir that would make her and her family famous was published and she made her intentions clear from the off. This was not, she wrote in the prologue, a piece of frivolous entertainment, but a 'canticle of love and gratitude to the Heavenly Father and his Divine Providence'. There was much quoting of St Ambrose, 'one of the greatest men of the fourth century', and as well as the family's dramatic flight from the Nazis, there were less dramatic scenes of them enjoying wonderful evenings together, reading the Gospels, which Maria got under way by inviting them to 'Come! Enter into eternal joy.' The book found a publisher and on the back of the fan base that the Trapp Family Singers had established over ten years of concert tours, became a modest bestseller.

If you skip over the hard-core passages about the meaning of Easter, the book is a very good read and fascinating when held up against the film version, about which Maria and her family were understandably ambivalent. Its blend of fact and fiction affronted them and the music of Rodgers and Hammerstein was not entirely to their taste.

The biographical foundations of *The Sound of Music* are broadly accurate. It is true that Maria was a scatterbrained novice at Nonnberg Abbey; it is true that the Mother Superior – who before taking any action did indeed enquire of herself, 'Is it the Will of God?' – thought she should see a bit of life and so posted her to the house of a Captain von Trapp, a widower who lived with his seven children in a mansion on the outskirts of Salzburg.

The captain was indeed a former officer in the Austrian Imperial

Navy, who had fought in the Boxer rebellion in China and been the first, wrote Maria proudly, 'to sense the importance of the submarine in warfare'. His first wife, Agathe, had been the granddaughter of Robert Whitehead, British inventor of the torpedo, whom he met when she christened his submarine. She died of scarlet fever shortly after the First World War. As in the film, the captain was so devastated by this that he retreated into himself and was shy with the children because they reminded him of her. He did summon them by whistle.

When Maria came to the door of his house, it really was in a ridiculous hat, the rim of which kept falling over her eyes, and she really did mistake Hans, the butler, for the captain.

The names of the children were different from those used in the film. In real life they were Maria, Johanna, Martina, Hedwig, Agathe, Rupert and Werner. When Maria arrived as governess she really was the twenty-sixth in a row and she succeeded where the others had failed because of the fun and energy she brought to the house. Against their father's wishes, she got them out of sailor suits and into play clothes and let them play volleyball on the lawn. Maria didn't customize the curtains to do this. Instead, she sat down and did what she always did in a tight spot, wrote to the Christ Child, asking Him for woollen mittens, hobnailed boots and a *wetterfleck*, a sort of woollen cape with a hood.

More than their wardrobe, however, what concerned Maria about the children was their ignorance of Austrian folk songs. When she arrived, the only songs they seemed to know were the national anthem and 'Silent Night'. She picked up her guitar and set about rectifying this. When the captain joined in the family singalong, accurately depicted in the film as a breakthrough in his emotional range and connection with the children, it was not with a quick verse from a folk ballad, but all twenty-two verses of 'In Dulci Jubilo', which he performed while accompanying himself on the violin.

The captain at this point was still planning to marry, not a baroness, but a princess called Yvonne, who, after observing the family together, really did say to her governess rival, 'Do you realize that the captain is in love with you?' The princess didn't want the children at the wedding and proposed to send the girls to a convent and the boys to a Jesuit college. Horrified, Maria packed and left.

The captain meanwhile realized that he was in love with her. He tried to make his intentions clear by buying her a gift, *The Golden Book for Housewives: A Guide Through the Year, Together With Five Hundred Recipes and One Thousand Advices*. But Maria was blind to his true meaning and so on the eve of his engagement to Princess Yvonne he sent her a cheeky note – 'I wish I could see your eyes when you read the announcement of my engagement' – to which she tartly replied, 'My eyes are none of your business.' He broke off his engagement to make them his business and asked Maria to marry him. She ran to the Reverend Mother for advice and wept when told it was the Will of God that she marry von Trapp; it turns out that she did, really, want to be a nun. In 1927, they married. Maria was twenty.

This all happened ten years before the film set it, which was just before the Anschluss in 1938, by which time in real life they'd had another two children, Rosmarie and Eleonore; a further son, Johannes, would be born in America. There was no Uncle Max, but the soprano Lotte Lehmann who overheard them singing one day in the garden and encouraged them to perform in public, although, as Maria pointed out, God was the only audience they needed. 'Music,' wrote Maria, 'what a powerful instrument, what a mighty weapon!' They also needed the money; for the wealthy captain had lost all his assets when the Austrian bank he had patriotically moved them to from England folded. 'On top of all his worries, I was getting on his nerves too!' If there is something Julie Andrews captured of the real Maria in her performance, it was this hearty, guileless tone. The Trapp Family Singers entered the folk competition, although their choral repertoire did not culminate in a charming spin on the children's song 'Tea with jam, jam and bread, jam and bread', but in a programme that included 'Alle Psallite', an organum from the sixteenth century, the Bach chorale 'Wie Schön Leuchtet der Morgenstern' and Telemann's extremely difficult trio sonata for two recorders and a spinet. Edelweiss is not a traditional Austrian folk song, but does, at least, grow in the Alps. They won the competition.

There, history and the film part company. The von Trapp family did not flee that night over the mountains. They left the country by train, in 1938, partly because the captain had been summoned for duty on a Nazi submarine and partly because he and his family were summoned to sing before Hitler on his birthday. Their objection to these duties had as much to do with their Austrian nationalism as disapproval of the Third Reich, or as Maria put it rather scarily, 'We learned that the love for your homeland comes even before the love for your family.' Their family motto was, 'Nec Aspera Terrent' – 'Nothing difficult frightens thee.'

The After-Life

When they got to New York, the von Trapps hoped to make some money with their singing. They were penniless at this point and it was all rather precarious. Maria went to see theatrical managers Messrs Schang and Coppicus, a division of Columbia Artists specializing in classical music acts. The artists on their books included concert pianist Maryla Jonas, a piano double act called Vronsky and Babin and the Leonard de Paur Infantry Chorus. Mr Coppicus enjoyed the Trapp Family Singers' programme of highbrow madrigals and complex choral arrangements but took one look at their clothes and exploded. Of course, Maria wasn't a movie star but a good, solid, Austrian woman, with Princess Leia braids at the side of her head and such extraordinarily grim taste in dirndls that the wardrobe department at 20th Century Fox had to tone down their authenticity for the film.

After marrying she did not develop a sudden affinity for stylish two-piece travel suits, but continued to wear traditional Austrian dress, even in America. Mr Coppicus went nuts at what he called their 'quaint ancient tunes' and fumed, 'You come and go like a funeral procession! No charming smile, no good looks either! Those long skirts, high necks, hair parted in the middle, braids in the back, shoes like boys', cotton stockings? Can't you get decent store clothes so one can see your legs in nylon stockings? Can't you get pretty, high-heeled shoes and put a little red on your lips?'

'No,' replied Maria von Trapp coldly. 'We can't.'

Without making any of the changes Mr Coppicus asked for, the von Trapps started to tour the country in a bus. Their repertoire went down like a bucket of cold water with American audiences. For their first concert in New York, they chose the three hardest madrigals they knew and devoted the second half to the entire 45-minute performance of 'Jesu Meine Freude'. The classical music press loved it but much of the audience left before the end.

Then they went to Los Angeles, where, writes Maria, with touching understatement, 'we didn't fit in very well'. Even she had begun to feel a little sorry for their audiences.

The turning point finally came in Denver, Colorado, where, while taking a deep breath before yodelling, Maria swallowed a fly on stage. She turned a bright shade of purple, held her breath for as long as she could and eventually did the only thing possible: burst into laughter. To her surprise, she found that the audience laughed with her and that her performance from that moment on was much more enthusiastically received. The family von Trapp learned to lighten up.

Returning to New York, they reauditioned for Schang and Coppicus and were signed on the spot.

For the next few years the family toured almost constantly. They did well enough to get their picture in *Life* magazine. Eventually they tired of travelling and bought a farm in Vermont, but had to go on the road again to meet the mortgage payments. Interest in them had waned and there was only one booking, in Bethlehem, Pennsylvania. It was make or break for the von Trapps. They pulled it out of the hat with Brahms's 'The Day Has Come When Thou And I, Dearest One, Must Say Goodbye', which had the audience in tears.

They returned to the farm to play volleyball, pray and make maple syrup. They set up the Trapp Family Music Camp. In May 1947, the captain died of cancer, aged sixty-seven. He was buried on a hill overlooking the farm, beneath a large wooden cross and his old U-boat flag. Maria, indomitable as ever, turned the farm into Cor Unum (from Cor Unum Et Anima Una, 'They were one heart and soul'), a Christian community. She wrote follow-ups to her successful book, including *Around the Year with the Trapp Family* and *A Family on Wheels: Further Adventures of the Trapp Family Singers*.

After the film was made, whenever the real von Trapps appeared in public, they were plagued with requests for 'Edelweiss'. Finally they buckled under public pressure and recorded some 'modern' music including a version of 'Waltzing Matilda', which threw into relief the value of their original programme. With the classical rolled R on 'drrrrink' and 'tuckerrr', their attempts to grapple with the words 'billabong' and 'jolly swag man', and the shrieking climax, like a subway train taking a corner, their performance of 'Waltzing Matilda' is one of the strangest recordings ever made. It was arranged, like all their songs, by an old friend of theirs from Salzburg, the Reverend Mr Franz Wasner, and appears on the CD *Folk Music Of Many Lands (Vol. II)*. Other tracks on the CD include some truly awesome yodelling and that Trio Sonata in F for two recorders and a spinet. Also a Hawaiian farewell song called 'Aloha Oe', which Hawaiian fans of *The Sound of Music* will find puzzling, as indeed Mexicans will be stumped by Mr Wasner's arrangement of 'Que Lejos Estoy' and Texans by 'The Lone Prairie' ('the lone prrrairrreee').

Maria died in 1987, aged eighty-two, and was buried next to her husband, on the hill overlooking the farm, where the von Trapp lodge still operates under the management of her descendants.

The Sound of Music is not like other musicals. It has strange powers to mortify and exult. It means more to some people than perhaps it deserves and incites greater hatred than its faults can be blamed for. I have a friend who says she could only marry a man who liked, or, more realistically, didn't actively loathe, *The Sound of Music*, because, while most of the time she isn't watching it, when she is it gladdens her heart like nothing on earth. There are probably statistics to show that, as with the number of rats in London, one is never further than five hundred yards from an amateur production of *The Sound of Music*. Its fans seem to treat it less as a film than a utility and it's almost impossible to get through a twelve-month period without inadvertently watching it. Traditionally it comes on TV on New Year's Day, when you are at your most vulnerable. Prone, still sweating champagne from the night before, you reach for the remote control, but your limbs won't obey and you fumble with the hand set and before you can switch channels those opening notes have sounded, dribs and drabs of flute like an offhand but irresistible invitation to come! Enter into eternal joy!

What Would Barbra Do?

The camera soars over the Alps and Maria runs across the mountainside. All it needs is a voiceover from Alan Whicker to look like a 1970s introduction to holiday homes in the Tyrol, but even though its naked resolve to uplift should be enough to put you right off, like those Christian prayers masquerading as non-denominational 'motivational' messages you find printed on cards and hung in spa waiting rooms, before you know it you're two hours in and hissing at the baroness as she clumsily tries to play ball with the children and the hills are alive with the sound of music whatever that means, but still, for some reason, it's impossible to get up and turn the thing off.

The fans

Because of the diversity of its fans, it is assumed that *The Sound of Music* works on a number of levels. If you have ever sat in a cinema wearing lederhosen or dressed as a brown paper package; if you have sniggered when, during the nuns' conference over Maria's whereabouts, Sister Margueretta says, 'Have you tried the barn? You know how much she adores the animals'; if you have watched as Christopher Plummer stands backlit in a doorway looking puzzled and aggrieved – which is most of the time – and imagined he is thinking I turned down King Lear for this – if you do all of this, then you are thought to be one sort of fan. If you don't, another.

The hardest of the hard-core *Sound of Music* fans hang out in their own chat rooms, where they exchange notes about the amateur productions they are taking part in and argue with you over interpretations of the film. Someone will post a message such as: 'Auditioning for Louisa, I'm a mezzo-soprano, what should I sing???'

'Try something mid-ranged,' someone else will reply, 'like "Sixteen Going on Seventeen",' while others will counter, 'I thought "Sixteen Going on Seventeen" was rather sopranic? I wouldn't say it was mid-ranged.'

The comment about the sopranic nature of 'Sixteen Going on Seventeen' was posted on the site by a contributor with the tag-line 'purr purr, me loves cats'. She went on to advise the auditionee not to try anything 'belty'.

'Exasperated sigh,' a further respondent posted, and re-commended 'something sweet and childish'. This sparked a separate debate around the question, 'Do you think it is possible for a high school student to play five-year-old Gretl?'

Someone with the tag-line 'preparing for auditions *On Golden Pond*,' replied, 'It's possible, but I think it would affect the show in a bad way, making it seem unrealistic, unless you are three feet tall.'

This really wound up Broadway Grl who wrote in response, 'I'm barely five foot three and I just played Maria.' She believed Maria's top note to be a G, but asked not to be quoted on that.

Someone else made the point: 'Maria shouldn't be judged by height, she should be judged by her talent.'

'Well, it's just my opinion,' huffed Golden Pond, 'but rarely can one find a set of von Trapp kids who are talented *and* look their age. When I was in *The Sound of Music*, Maria, Liesl and Friedrich were all the same size, but Maria wore heels, which doesn't work too well because nuns don't wear high heels.'

The original contributor then resurfaced. 'Thanks for everyone's help!!!' she wrote. 'Unfortunately, my mom wouldn't let me audition in the end, so I didn't try out, however I'm planning on auditioning for *A Chorus Line*, so wish me luck on that!'

'What is your mother's problem anyway?' wrote Golden Pond. 'Is she some sort of right wing anti-arts woman?'

'Ha ha no,' replied the student. 'She's just concerned about my grades (I am an A-student). I'm definitely going to audition for *ACL*. I'm excited but nervous too ... but hey, what's the worst that can happen? Make a fool of myself? Haha.'

The discussion eventually broke up with a posting by WickedWitch, who wrote, 'I love how art is subjective!'

The philosophy

I have never liked *The Sound of Music*, although, like everyone else, I seem to know every word of it by heart. It is as if we were born with the lyrics hard-wired to our brains and there is nothing to be done but to try to understand them.

Although it was written by sophisticated people in sophisticated cities, what *The Sound of Music* promotes is the idea of the authentic self: the state of grace that we all existed in before we started studying our own reactions to things or were exposed to advertising. The unfettered translation of impulse into action is the musical's high ideal and any self-respecting heroine must act on instinct, must be 'true to herself'. Maria von Trapp is no exception. She confirms what we have always suspected: that the apparently selfish ethos of the musical is actually God's Will in disguise. It isn't selfish at all – it's self*less*! It is Maria's stated aim in both the book and the film 'to find out what is the Will of God and do it whole-heartedly' and it turns out – what are the chances? – that what God wants is for her to behave like the traditional heroine of a musical: to be demure but ambitious; to maintain behind her cheery demeanour a backbone of steel; to rationalize her fears without denying their existence; to fall in love with an unsuitable man who Needs a Lot of Work but is none the less worthwhile. To enter a singing competition – and to win!

Accompanying the idea of the authentic self is the other key philosophy of *The Sound of Music*, that of More Than You Know. More Than You Know is like Appearing Not To Try, but with integrity.

'More than you know,' says the captain, gazing up at Maria as she ascends the stairs. He has just had his watershed moment harmonizing with the children. Through her unworldly actions she has achieved more than all the scheming baronesses in the world. (As I grow older, I sympathize more and more with the baroness in this arrangement.) Natural goodness has won out, like Cyd Charisse's simple charms in *Brigadoon* winning out over Gene Kelly's smart fiancée. More Than You Know is the film-maker's equivalent of Marie Antoinette's trip to the peasant's cottage in the garden: the romance of simplicity; the fantasy of innocence.

The captain falls in love with Maria despite himself; she falls in love with him despite herself. She is beautiful but she doesn't know it;

he is sensitive but he doesn't know it. Nobody ever seems to know what they're doing or why, and it's infuriating. Maria tells the baroness she's done nothing to make herself attractive to the captain and the baroness laughs her tinkly laugh. 'But you don't have to, my dear,' she says. It is the Will of God. The Reverend Mother chips in at this point with a hearty sermon about responsibility and sings 'Climb Ev'ry Mountain' with great gusto and a nail-biting ascent to top C in the final verse.

It is from Christopher Plummer that the seditious undercurrents in the film are thought to flow. While the genius of Julie Andrews's performance is her straight delivery, Plummer's strength is his humour, the look on his face when Maria says at the dinner table, 'Excuse me, Captain, haven't we forgotten to thank the Lord?' There has never been a more sardonic delivery of 'Amen' in film history. Plummer is the great-grandson of Canadian prime minister Sir John Abbott, who trained as a concert pianist before going into the theatre. He did Ibsen in '59, Hamlet in '64, Oedipus the King in '67. He played Jason in *Medea* and was part of the National Theatre under Laurence Olivier and the RSC under Peter Hall. His role as the captain in *The Sound of Music*, or the Sound of Mucus as he called it, was at such odds with his background that he claims to have been drunk every night of the eleven-week location shoot, just as a way of coping.

Plummer is often blamed for sending up the film. But he is too good an actor for this. Without his ironic air the captain would be a very dull and stuffy hero. Plummer's realization that he's in love with Maria has the same force to it as the scene in *My Fair Lady* when gruff old Rex Harrison overcomes obstacles in his own nature to realize that he's in love with Eliza. Many years after *The Sound of Music* was released, Plummer admitted that, despite his grousing, it really wasn't that bad a film. 'It is sentimental,' he said. 'But sentimental' – he paused, to think – 'sentimental in the *right way*.'

Everything you need to know about *The Sound of Music* you learn in the first five minutes, when Maria journeys from the abbey to the house singing 'I Have Confidence'. It sounds like a line from the Moonie manifesto, but underneath its maddening hippy sentiments it has quite a kick. Andrews's talent is to deliver a sappy line with just a hint of anger, a steel coat that implies it takes some nerve to be such a Pollyanna. In the course of five minutes the song moves between fear, confidence, self-assurance, doubt and eventual resolve. It shows how small failures of nerve can take three verses of internal cheerleading to chase off – telephone phobia, for example, or seeing the ground unexpectedly yawn open during small talk at a party or, in Maria's case, getting out of bed with anything less than full gratitude to God for the gift of existence. It is the sort of song people listen to before they go to a job interview or on a first date or out in the rain, their anxiety the size of the Alps as they appear in the window of the bus that takes Maria from the abbey. All musicals are concerned with closing the gap between who we are and who we want to be; but the good ones occasionally acknowledge the shortfall.

A friend of mine recently discovered that her therapist had never seen the film and that for two years she had been entrusting her emotional welfare to a woman who didn't understand the steering influence of all this. She suspended all further sessions until her therapist had bought the DVD and got stuck into studying it.

The Tour

If there is any place in the world more at odds with the joy – no, the *gladness* – of *The Sound of Music*, it is Salzburg on a Sunday morning in mid-winter. The runway at Salzburg airport cleaves through the snow alongside wooden chalets that look like giant cuckoo clocks. The lavatories in the terminal building are spotless. 'Very efficient,' you observe guiltily, and snigger.

Poor Austrians. It seems a final, intractable punishment for the Second World War that to large parts of the world, their history should boil down to the exploits of a pantomime baron, a singing nun and seven American-accented children. (Actually, Friedrich, the oldest boy, has a stab at an English accent, but by the time you get down the line to five-year-old Gretl, it's all gone a bit Shirley Temple.) One day, a friend and I get up at 4 a.m. to catch a flight from Luton airport to Salzburg, to go on one of the tours. Such is the intensity of competition in the city that it only costs thirty-five euros. We get a cab from the airport to the Alter Markt, a traditional cobbled square through which Austrians in ankle-length fur are taking their Sunday walk. We find a traditional Austrian café and are served by a woman in a French maid's uniform who, to our delight, behaves in a manner we construe to be traditionally Austrian. 'Sit!' she barks, as we idle over the cake display. We sit. We order strudel. We pay and walk to the Christmas market that sells outsized chocolate pretzels and wooden tree decorations and hats with flaps made out of fur. We cross the Salzach river on an iron bridge that features in the film's 'Do-Re-Mi' sequence, but after we have taken a few snow-blurred photos it proves too cold to linger. It is the sort of bright, clear day when you breathe in and the air tastes of toothpaste. After lunch, as instructed, we locate the fibreglass cow and wait.

The cow is parked beside a wooden ticket booth, slightly to the right and in front of Salzburg's cathedral, so that worshippers emerging into the dazzling winter morning must put a small, discernible effort into ignoring it. On its flanks are painted scenes from the film in which Maria's hair has come up orange and the grass of the meadow that electric green used by insects to advertise their deadliness. We hang at a distance, trying to look as if we might be in town to visit Mozart's birthplace, or Salzburg's famous puppet theatre, or the city's fifteenth-century bull organ, 'still blowing strong after five hundred years', as Charmian Carr, the actress who plays Liesl, puts it in the behind-the-scenes documentary. Some teenagers arrive and throw themselves over the cow with unselfconscious joy. Then the bus pulls up and we shuffle on board and try to get a measure of the others in the group.

In the seats behind us are some very loud, very camp, youngish men who announce they are from Kentucky and immediately start singing 'Do-Re-Mi', except one, who slouches in his seat and goes instantly to sleep. His breath rolls over the headrest in an alcoholic cloud. There are some English-looking couples in beige waterproof outerwear. There are Japanese teenage girls in bright bobble hats.

What Would Barbra Do?

There are some dowdier British teenagers and then some American girls who judging by their chatter are on the final leg of a European tour.

'It's this place where a volcano erupted and all this ash came down and everyone died?'

'No way.'

'Yuh, they were totally burned to death.'

'No way.'

'Yuh.'

At the front of the bus stands a woman. She is British and her expression is hard to read: somewhere between forbearance and despair. She is called Sue and is from Bromley in south London. 'Many of you,' she says, 'will have waited for this moment for a very long time. And now . . . here it is.'

The mood on the bus is a little tense at this stage, as everyone bar the Kentuckians tries to figure out where they fit in and whether, when it comes to the advertised 'group singalong', they will be able to carry it off.

'How do you solve a problem like Maria?' asks Sue, as the bus pulls away from the kerb.

'Therapy!' someone cries.

'I don't know about Maria,' says Sue, ignoring him, which clears up any doubts about the elasticity of her script, 'but Ted's been trying to solve a problem like Sue for the last eight years . . . and he's no nearer to cracking it!' Ted stares stonily at the road ahead. 'He's Austrian,' she says, sotto voce.

The Sound of Music

After driving past the Mirabel gardens, where the children ran around the Pegasus statue in their curtain costumes, the bus stops outside the great house itself: Leopoldskron Castle. The car park is loaded with coaches trying to reverse without flattening stray fans, while dislodging great blobs of snow from the overhead branches. They fall with a soft thud to the icy ground.

The tour used to go right up to the perimeter fence of the house, but that stopped after visitors repeatedly stole off to climb over it; the presence of the gazebo on the other side was too great a temptation. Now the gazebo has been moved to a neutral location and the closest you can get to the house is half a mile away, over water. Sue tells us that during the filming of the scene in which the children fall out of their rowing boat into the lake, the smallest child, Gretl, nearly drowned. She tells us that the interiors weren't shot here but at a studio in Los Angeles. She tells us that 'The Lonely Goatherd' was not, originally, supposed to play during the puppet show, but during the storm.

'So where was "My Favourite Things" supposed to go?'

'In the abbotry,' says Sue. 'With the nuns.'

Everybody screams.

I walk with Sue back to the coach. She tells me she came to Austria ten years ago. She used to be in regular tourism, but as an English speaker in Salzburg it was inevitable, she says, that she would one day wind up on a *Sound of Music* tour. She has done the tour twice a day, five days a week, for the last eight years, which explains why when she's reciting the script the cadences of her English rise and fall like Chinese: she has lost all sense of its meaning.

What Would Barbra Do?

'Do you love *The Sound of Music*?' I ask.

After a long pause she says, 'I've learned to. My mother hated it. Funny.' She looks at the snowy landscape. 'It brings happiness to so many people; it's nice to be a part of that.'

What the *Sound of Music* tour has done to Ted is anyone's guess. Behind his mirrored shades he says nothing, but stares silently at the road ahead. Over the course of the day I develop a fantasy in which, pushed too far one day by Sue's manic cheerfulness, he takes out an axe and slowly, expressionlessly, hacks everyone on the bus to death, sinking the blade into Sue's skull while humming a few bars from 'Edelweiss'.

'How do we know it's the same gazebo?'

We are standing in a semicircle before a many-sided glass structure that looks as if it was installed after a successful telephone pitch by Anglia Windows. It is in the grounds of a National Trust type property, Hellbrunn Castle, the second stop on the tour, where visitors can view it under the proper supervision. Sue is orchestrating a photo session.

'No, *wait*,' she says to the Japanese girls, who have failed to understand the rota system that allows everyone to get a shot of themselves alone in front of the gazebo. They have barged in on the English couple who say 'Um?' and look at Sue. Sue explains that until a few years ago you could actually go inside the gazebo, but then an 86-year-old woman broke her hip jumping off a bench while re-enacting 'I Am Sixteen Going on Seventeen', there was talk of a lawsuit, and since then you can only view it from the outside. Personally, the scene in the gazebo gives me the creeps, but lots of people cite it as their favourite of the film. Rolfe's reticence, Liesl's eagerness; his delivery boy uniform, her floaty dress; his tutorial in current affairs: 'Some people think we ought to be German. They're very mad at those who don't think so.' Her telegram: 'Dear Rolfe. Stop. Don't stop. Your Liesl.' Yuk. Rolfe sings in a weird falsetto and tries to show off to Liesl how sophisticated he is, telling her she's just a child and that adult matters are beyond her ken; meanwhile she's chasing him round the gazebo like Benny Hill. 'No, Liesl,' he says sternly, 'we mustn't.'

'Why not, silly?'

But she is merely expressing her authentic self.

'How do we know it's the same gazebo?' I ask.

Sue looks at me as if I have asked how we know the earth is round. 'Because there is a plaque,' she says.

It is starting to snow.

There are two further stops on the tour, one at the Mondsee cathedral, where the wedding scene was filmed, and the other at the base of the mountain. We pad into the cathedral in total darkness, unable to find the light switch. The temperature by now is well below freezing. The two British teens kneel in front of the altar to commune with their idols. 'Look!' shout the Kentuckians. 'Austria's first same-sex marriage!' The girls frown. We eat more strudel in a nearby café and from there it is a long drive across country to the Salzkammergut lake district and the beautiful village at the foot of the mountain, on the rim of Lake Wolfgang, where the exterior shots of the escape were filmed. The ground is hard with packed ice. 'Don't imagine,' says Sue, 'that if you'd fled this way during the war you'd have found safety. No. Because over this mountain doesn't lie Switzerland. Over this mountain' – she pauses – 'lies Germany.' Several people gasp. Sue smiles. 'And not only Germany, but Bavaria, home . . . of Hitler.'

'Oh, my!'

We crunch along to the gift shop where you can buy tea towels, CDs of the Trapp Family Singers put out by Trapp Family Lodge Inc., and traditional Austrian hats. We try on the hats.

The film's climax is the von Trapp family's flight from the Nazis, which kicks off when Herr Zeller, formerly their neighbour, now their oppressor, greets them at the gate and escorts them to the folk festival, a scene that required two thousand extras to fill the amphitheatre. It is usually the heroine of the musical who stands centre stage at the end, looking ravaged. But in this case it's the captain, who breaks down during his performance of 'Edelweiss': 'I know you share this love. I pray you will never let it die.' The family chips in to rescue him and the audience follows suit. Beneath their moustaches, the mouths of the Nazis involuntarily twitch. When Uncle Max thanks them for their performance, he says, 'Even now, officials are waiting in the auditorium to escort Captain von Trapp to his new command in the naval forces' – pregnant pause – 'of the *Third Reich*.' In the audience a man grumbles, 'Third Reich,' as you might expect Alan Titchmarsh to grumble 'Damn slugs' while reviewing a devastated salad patch.

'They're gone!' calls the Nazi, emerging from the tunnel. Someone blows a whistle. A Scooby-Doo type chase ensues. The family hides in the convent. As Sister Margueretta fumbles to open the gate, Herr Zeller hisses, 'Hurry up, woman,' a useful reminder, should anyone need it; Nazis: no respect for nuns. The nuns save the day! They have tampered with the Nazi-mobile! In the final shot, the family are seen walking up the mountain, the captain with Gretl in his arms. It isn't actually the same girl who played Gretl in the rest of the film, however. Christopher Plummer got the hump at having to lift such a large child, so they replaced her in the closing scene with a smaller one. 'That,' says Sue, almost panting at this stage, 'is why you can't see her face.'

We get back on the coach. A laminated photo is passed around of the actors who played the von Trapp children, now grown up and captured in Salzburg on a recent reunion. People try to take pictures of it, but each time the flash reflects off the glossy surface and ruins the shot. We are given a free packet of edelweiss seeds.

As Austria slides by outside there comes, at last, the much advertised singalong. Over the coach tannoy a tinny recording of the soundtrack plays. 'High on a hill was a lonely goatherd.' The boys from Kentucky sing along lustily, everyone else mumbles. 'Take it away, Ted!' says Sue.

Ted flips the overhead lights on and off a few times.

Exit Song

Exit Song

A parcel arrived in the mail one day, addressed to my mother and with a note from her friend David attached. 'When you said on the phone that you were trying to remember the song about Elsie Down in Chelsea (how gallant of you) and I was able to tell you that it is from *Cabaret*, I thought you might like to have it. So here it is.'

Elsie Down in Chelsea was my mother's name for the title song from *Cabaret*, which she admired for its robust take on Elsie's demise. It is unclear, from the song, whether Elsie actually dies as a result of 'pills and liquor', or whether this is just shorthand for the kind of life she had led. But my mother thought she had broadly the right idea; if one achieved nothing else in life, one might at least hope to scandalize the neighbours.

The version David sent was copied from an LP onto tape and was not from the film version, but a rare recording of the 1968 London stage show starring a young Judi Dench as Sally Bowles and Barry Dennen as the emcee. Dennen, if you are unfamiliar with him, is a New York veteran of musical theatre who played Pontius Pilate in the 1973 film version of *Jesus Christ Superstar*. (His website is a tribute to the guts and perseverance required to survive in the world of musical theatre. As he notes in his biography, after he appeared in Stanley Kubrick's *The Shining* in 1980 things went a little quiet and he has more recently 'played a small role in James Cameron's blockbuster movie *Titanic*, as a praying man being hurried along by Leonardo DiCaprio' and is currently 'very active doing voiceovers for video games, including the voice of FatMan in the hugely successful video game Metal Gear Solid II'. He is a one-time boyfriend and nightclub promoter of Barbra Streisand and his book, *My Life With Barbra: A Love Story*, comes with a citation on the dust jacket by Joan Rivers, who says, 'I can't recommend it enough.')

The idea of someone making my mother a mix tape made me smile. I hadn't made one myself since I was a teenager recording all those chart shows off Radio 1, trying to reform my music taste and thinking I was getting one over the system. Mix tapes that you make for someone else are the boy's emotional response to things, a way of saying tangentially what can't be said outright. In this case they were an act of friendship the nature of which was immediately and implicitly understood.

As well as the title track, the tape contained all the other songs from the stage production, including 'Don't Tell Mama', which was replaced in the film by 'Mein Herr', a shame, I think, because the former is funnier and saucier.

Dench is miscast in some ways; she has such a hearty Englishness about her that any attempt to be seedy just comes off as jolliness. But maybe that was true of Isherwood's original character, too. There is something about that kind of Englishness that precludes vulnerability. It speaks of rebellion from a world that will still be there when the rebel tires of bohemia and wants to go back. In the film version Minnelli seemed more precariously situated, a real exile. Perhaps this is the wisdom of hindsight, but you saw something unhinged in her that Dench was too forthright to carry off.

The landlady gets many more songs in the stage production, in keeping with her central role in the book. In fact, as W. H. Auden told Isherwood, if there is a moral to the tale it is about the general indestructibility of landladies and artists. In this recording the landlady was played by Lila Kedrova, the Russian actress who won an Oscar for her role as Madame Hortense in *Zorba the Greek*. She is the soul of *Cabaret*, a woman who has been tossed about by history and tried to keep in with whomever one needs to keep in with, whilst maintaining some kind of core self-belief. She croaks, 'Vhen you are as old as I – is anyone as old as I?' and laughs mercilessly in a way that echoes all through the show. She sings a number at the end called 'Who Cares' in which she bellows, over and over, 'who cares, who cares, who cares'. It has the opposite to the intended effect; all you can hear in her voice is care, like a foghorn, warning ships off the rocks.

There was room at the end of the tape for some other songs, so David had recorded Lotte Lenya doing two Brecht/Kurt Weill numbers in her tightly sprung voice: they were 'Mack the Knife' from *The Threepenny Opera* and 'Alabama Song' in which she growls, 'Show me the way to the next whisky bar.' Then a very English-accented Jessie Matthews singing 'Three Wishes', her vibrato so out of control that it sounded sort of corrugated, like a stick being dragged along railings. Then an extraordinary, scratchy recording of a scene from the 1938 film *The Great Waltz* ('Your beating heart, your pounding pulse will tell you it's the most exciting musical love story ever told!') in which Miliza Korjus, the Berlin nightingale, is mistaken for Mrs Strauss when she is in fact his mistress. She rides with him in a carriage and improvises the chorus to 'Tales from the Vienna

Woods' in time to the beat of the wheels. 'Oh, it's so beautiful, Mrs Strauss,' says a passing peasant. 'What's the name of it?'

'That? Oh, it's called . . . it's called . .' She sighs, saddened by the peasant's error and by the wistful tone of the music. 'It's called "Tales from the Vienna Woods".'

Korjus crushed her leg in a car accident while she was preparing to make her second film, with Robert Taylor and Hedy Lamarr, and retreated to Mexico, where she shot the only other film she would appear in, *Imperial Chivalry*, in 1942. She carried on giving concerts after moving back to Los Angeles. Joan Sutherland was apparently a great admirer of hers. She married a Dr Walter Shector and died of heart failure in 1980. 'She was very beautiful, in a sort of slightly massive way,' wrote David in his letter. Her first line in the film was, 'Yunk man, you are standink on mai dress.'

Korjus was rumoured to have been able to hit the C above top C and there is a frightening bit in the middle when she sings like a kettle and you think she might actually make it. Her voice is so high that you can't place it on the scale, like when water is very hot you sometimes can't tell if it's hot or if it's cold.

Another mix tape followed in the post. It had lots of songs from the backstage musicals. We listened to them in the kitchen and then in the living room and then, when we weren't moving around much any more, in the downstairs bedroom. I made my mother a tape, too, and with a masochism I find hard to understand now but which seemed funny at the time, put lots of songs about death on it.

Exit Song

Fuck it; let the air in.

So we had 'Pore Jud is Daid' from *Oklahoma!*, and not one but two versions of 'Send in the Clowns' and 'Ol' Man River'. We had Beatrice Lillie doing Noel Coward's 'The Party's Over Now'.

The nurses came. They suggested that instead of food my mother eat frozen pineapple chunks. She gave them pitying looks. 'Give us a smile!' said one. My mother said, 'I'll smile on the condition you don't come to see me again.'

Another nurse came and my mother deftly extracted her life story and started calling letting agents on her behalf.

In the evenings, we worked our way systematically through *The Savoy Cocktail Book*, compiled in 1930 by legendary barman Harry Craddock and accompanied by beautiful art deco illustrations and in later editions an advisory note suggesting Pernod as a good substitute for absinthe. When Craddock was asked how best to drink a cocktail, he said 'quickly'. We figured White Russians were at least as nutritious as frozen pineapple chunks.

'The elephant is ringing,' my mother said. And 'If that beaky bees next door comes and snucks her head in, tell her to go away.' The word 'hospital' became 'bottle'. Jacket became 'jerkin' and then 'jifkin'. She asked what time the film *Hairless in Seattle* began and we looked at each other, startled, then cracked up laughing and poured another drink. 'I had a funny worm last night,' she said.

'Dream.'

'I had a funny dream. That's what I said.'

*

What Would Barbra Do?

Another tape arrived, number three, with Nelson Eddy doing the Indian Love Call. 'High drama,' said my mother and rolled her eyes. There was Kay Thompson urging everyone to 'think pink', and Audrey Hepburn on how to be lovely. At some point in the summer she put on a white towelling turban, got in a wheelchair and in the manner of Norma Desmond embarked on a farewell tour of the village. We made our way up the street, meeting and greeting. I wasn't sure how much she was taking in at this stage. And then a woman we knew slightly charged over and tearfully clutched my mother's hand and my mother shot me a look that said help me out here, the woman is mad.

For the first time in her life she complained of being in pain. I was angry with her for acting out of character and tried to nudge her back into it. 'We mustn't be sad,' I said.

She gave me a cool look. 'Are you something in the medical profession?' She always knew when a style had stopped working for her.

I lay in the bed next to hers and put in my headphones to block out the sound of her breathing.

The songs about death became unbearable, the songs about life worse. What had once seemed joyful now seemed 'life-affirming', in the language of the obituaries. What had seemed fierce and celebratory seemed to protest too much. All that bellowing and hollering and rejecting of one's fate had an air of panic about it, like something sung in the face of its own contradiction. 'When I go, I'm going like Elsie . . .' Was it about rapture? 'When I go . . .' Was it about stoicism?

What a performance.

Although they claimed to teach one how to forbear the final

curtain, what they actually offered was an attitude towards life, the life already lived, and as such at this point had nothing more to offer.

Eventually we sat side by side on the bed in silence.

'Bloody fuck,' she said.

'I know.'

It was almost two years later that I finally got round to unpacking stuff from the sale of the house. I needed my birth certificate for something and the box of papers under the desk in my flat that I'd succeeded in ignoring for so long had finally to be gone through. There was a mountain of letters and photos and school reports; cuttings from newspapers with big crosses next to them, which my mother had marked for my interest. Shopping lists in her writing on the backs of envelopes. I don't know how half the stuff got in. It was as if we had fled the house at gunpoint and just grabbed at random whatever came to hand. Halfway through the box I found a brown envelope with some tapes in it. 'When you said on the phone that you were trying to remember the song about Elsie Down in Chelsea . . .'

I sat on the arm of the sofa and listened to them, feeling as each track started like Humphrey Bogart in *Casablanca*: 'I thought I told you never to play that song.' There was Lila Kedrova, creaking like a rusty door hinge. 'Vhen you are as old as I – is anyone as old as I?' And Miliza Korjus's C above top C. 'It's called . . . it's called "Tales from the Vienna Woods".' And Audrey Hepburn on how to be lovely. They didn't sound mocking any more. Just silly. As silly as you only are with the people you love.

Acknowledgements

Acknowledgements

Standing Ovation

Thanks first and foremost to my dad, for listening to me blah on about musicals well beyond the limits of his interest and for always having a well-stocked fridge. Thanks to Jat Gill, David Black, Deniz Erdem, Kate Fawcett, Hannah Pool and Ritchie Parrott for all their help and advice, musicals-related and otherwise; to Dee Rissik for lending me her beautiful house to write in; to Pat Kavanagh and Linda Evans for their patience and general excellence; to Ian Katz for so many years of the best editing in town. And to Merope Mills and Oliver Burkeman, for making this book and everything else in life, better.

Text Acknowledgements

In order of appearance, a list of books, films, musicals and websites I have mentioned, and the people who created them.

The Sound of Music (Dir: Robert Wise; music: Richard Rodgers; lyrics: Oscar Hammerstein II) 3, 17, 213, 217, 222, 225, 226, 233, 234, 235

Inferno (Motorhead) 10

Oliver! (Dir: Carol Reed; music: Lionel Bart) 27, 131

The King and I (Dir: Walter Lang; music: Richard Rodgers and Oscar Hammerstein II) 28, 29

8 Mile (Dir: Curtis Hanson) 30

My Fair Lady (Dir: George Cukor; music: Alan Jay Lerner; lyrics: Frederick Loewe) 34

Gigi (Dir: Vincente Minnelli; music: Alan Jay Lerner; lyrics: Frederick Loewe) 34, 108, 118

Acknowledgements

What Would Barbra Do?

Cover Credits

Julie Andrews in *Mary Poppins*, 1964, directed by Robert Stevenson: © Walt Disney Pictures/The Kobal Collection

Julie Andrews in *The Sound of Music*, 1965, directed by Robert Wise: © 20th Century Fox/The Kobal Collection

Judy Garland and Ray Bolger in *The Wizard of Oz*, 1939, directed by Victor Fleming: © MGM/The Kobal Collection

Jane Powell and Fred Astaire in *Royal Wedding*, 1951, directed by Stanley Donen: © MGM/The Kobal Collection

Liza Minnelli in *Cabaret*, 1972, directed by Bob Fosse: © ABC/Allied Artists/The Kobal Collection

Barbra Streisand in *Funny Girl*, 1968, directed by William Wyler: © Columbia/The Kobal Collection

Shirley MacLaine in *Sweet Charity*, 1969, directed by Bob Fosse: © Universal/The Kobal Collection

Cyd Charisse and Fred Astaire in *The Band Wagon*, 1953, directed by Vincente Minnelli: © MGM/The Kobal Collection